Myth or Miracle?

The Image of Guadalupe

Myth or Miracle?

REVISED EDITION

JODY BRANT SMITH

✝

IMAGE ☻ BOOKS

A Division of Doubleday & Company, Inc.

Garden City, New York

1984

Image Book edition published September 1984
by special arrangement with Doubleday & Co., Inc.

Grateful acknowledgment is made to the following for permission
to reprint their copyrighted material:

English translation by James A. Guest of "The Primitive Relation,"
reprinted by permission of Dr. Guest.

"The Codex Saville: America's Oldest Book" by Mariano Cuevas,
S.J., from *Historical Records and Studies*, vol. XIX (September
1929), copyright 1929 by U.S. Catholic Historical Society, reprinted with permission.

English translation of "The Nican Mopohua" from *Am I Not Here?*,
reprinted by permission of AMI International Press, Inc.

Photo #24, reprinted with permission of University of Texas Press.

Library of Congress Cataloging in Publication Data
Smith, Jody Brant, 1943–
The image of Guadalupe.
Bibliography: p. 000
Includes index.
1. Guadalupe, Our Lady of.   I. Title.
BT660.G8S44   1983   232.91'7'097253
ISBN 0-385-15971-4
Library of Congress Catalog Card Number: 80–2066

To Jody Bass and Gladys Patterson Smith, my parents

To Heather Deborah and Jody Brant II, my children, and

To MARIA

✠

the One and the Many

Contents

CONTENTS

Preface

BEFORE TURNING TO ONE OR TWO SUCCINCT THEORETICAL observations, I want to thank the many people whose contributions made this book possible. Omissions are inadvertent, and I ask the indulgence of anyone unrecognized.

My first thanks go to my friend Robert T. Heller, Executive Editor of the Religion Department of Doubleday. Bob was the first to encourage me in this project, and has never stopped, even during the difficult transition from scholarly monographs to inviting narrative. Moreover, his was a consistent voice of confidence within a larger framework of a world which all too often appears merely contentious. Also, I thank Theresa M. D'Orsogna and Mr. Heller's assistant, Ann Stephens, at Doubleday; and Marian Skedgill.

Naturally a great many people in Mexico have helped me in varied but important ways. Most of all, I particularly want to thank the always-helpful Cardinal Corripio-Ahumada, the Archbishop of Mexico City; as well as Abbot Schulenburg of the Basilica of Our Lady of Guadalupe and his staff, especially Mrs. López for translation assistance; and Monseñores Cervantes, Salazar, and Montemayor of the Center for Guadalupan Studies in Mexico City, each of whom has played a crucial role in a still-unfolding adventure. Others whose help was much appreciated are Mrs. Madrazo and her sister, and Mr. Ochoa, her cousin. Next, I wish to thank three gentlemen who have shared their basic research with me: ophthalmologist Dr. Torija, criminologist Dr. Palacios, and systems engineer Dr. Aste. All are excellent people, but I must reiterate my affection for the last two, since they additionally made available their automobiles and their homes.

Filial affection is the correct description of my feelings for my dear friend Dr. Philip Serna Callahan, professor of entomology at the University of Florida and a biophysicist with the United States Department of Agriculture. Like my initial contact with my editor, my relationship with Dr. Callahan was a rapport built on mutual faith.

My appreciation is also extended to several other friends: my college colleagues Dr. Consuelo Teichert, who not only translated old sources but also generously contributed in terms of letters and phone calls, and Dr. James A. Guest, multiple linguist, who translated the *Primitive Relation*, and my close friend Professor John Hofen and Mrs. Philomena Marshall, for their help with German sources. Mrs. Moger, who typed the *Nican*, I also thank.

The publication of this book occurs nearer four than three years after its beginning, due to the richness of the materials available. In early stages, friends such as Wayne Walden, Mae Chenier, Barbara Bullock and, in Canada, author Merle Shain were of great help as well as, later on, Mrs. Pearl Zaki, Ramiz and Lulu Gilada, and Mr. Harry John.

The Museum of the American Indian in New York City

allowed me to study what appears to be the oldest surviving pre-Columbian book, the Codex Saville. When photographs were not of good-enough quality for reproduction, the museum staff generously and without fee furnished me an excellent print of this most interesting artifact.

Finally, the promised theoretical observations—qualifications, more accurately. The Guadalupe vista is panoramic. I have tried to indicate in this work something of the surface and of the perimeters, but I have purposely avoided, in keeping with the nature of an introductory work, exploring the depths.

I believe that the burgeoning field of archaeoastronomy is highly relevant to the subject of Guadalupan origins, especially the immediately Mexican origins. In Chapter II, I have given some references that were found in four Aztec *anales* regarding the Image of Guadalupe. I have by choice excluded an extremely interesting reference date, 1556, and coordinated the Tepeyac apparition with that of another, the 1531 appearance of the stupendous Halley's Comet. The difference in the dating can be explained by the difficulty in reconciling the Aztec and European calendars and by the fact that in 1531 the Julian calendar, not our modern Gregorian, was in effect.

To the best of my knowledge, these points have not been made before.

Jody Brant Smith
October 1982

Preface to the Revised Edition

In the original preface I suggested that a new science —archaeoastronomy—is relevant to the matter of Guadalupan origins. I want now to clarify briefly that supposition, while also adding a few words of clarification regarding the difficult matter of dating the apparition.

In Chapter II (pp. 25–26) I list several anonymous sixteenth-century *anales* (yearbooks), each of which make note of the Mexican apparition of Our Lady of Guadalupe.

Here is another, particularly fascinating, account: "1556,12 *tecpatl: Descendió la Señora a Tepeyacac; en el mismo tiempo, humeó la estrella.*" [1556,12 *tecpatl:* Our Lady descended to Tepeyacac; at the same time, there came a smoking star.][1]

This source confirms the coincidental apparitions of Our Lady of Guadalupe and the periodic Halley's comet, in the year 1531 (see original Preface, p. xi). "Smoking star" is a rendering of the Spanish translation of the Nahuatl word *citlalimpopocal,* which means "comet."[2]

---

[1] G. Velazquez, cited in J. B. Ugarte, *Cuestiónes Históricas Guadalupanas* (Mexico City, 1946), p. 27.

[2] Anthony F. Aveni, *Skywatchers of Ancient Mexico* (Austin: University of Texas Press, 1980), pp. 27–28.

Several additional matters are noteworthy. A heretofore ignored section of the Codex Telleriano-Remensis (see Photograph 24) shows a dramatically accurate illustration of a solar eclipse, with a comet in the background. The arabic numerals are clearly visible as 1531.[3] This provides an independent confirmation for the date of Halley's comet. Taken with the yearbook entry citing both comet and Guadalupan apparition in the same period, we may infer that both events occured in the same year and that both were outstanding in the mind of the anonymous Aztec chronicler. The reader is asked to turn to Chapter II for an explanation of the anomalous dating of the years. The Indians did not immediately comprehend the European system of notation. This is immediately obvious in photograph 24, where we see a correction from "1548" to "1531." One encounters similar "drawn through" corrections on many Indian documents of the same early colonial period.

Other additions include sections on the radically alternative *Apologia del Dr. Mier,* which proposes an entirely different origin for the Guadalupe Image, and a critique by seventeenth-century Mexican scholar Bercero Tanco, together with related materials. These sections are added to the Appendices.

Within the book proper are expanded sections on the controversial "faces," etc., in the eye(s) of the Madonna and more "impossible coincidences" in Chapter III. The author considers the phenomenon of coincidence or syn-

[3.] Ibid., p. 9, Fig. B.

chronicity, to constitute the irreducible miracle of the Guadalupan experience.

Finally, point of clarification. Page xi incorrectly implies that the Julian calendar in effect in 1531 accounts for the dating inconsistencies. The significance of the Julian entry is that (a), as with the Halley's comet entry, the correspondence seems never to have been recognized before, and (b) the traditional date of the Guadalupan painting, December 12, cannot be correct. December 12, 1531 (Julian), corresponds by intercalation to December 22, 1531 (Gregorian), because, even by the sixteenth century, ten days of error had crept into the Julian system. One of several implications of this is again associated with archaeoastronomy: December 22 is at the time of the winter solstice. And of course we may observe that in the painting on the tilma, Our Lady occludes the sun.

List of Photographs

The Image of Guadalupe

I.
Our Lady
of
Guadalupe

> Like the virus which sleeps as a mineral for thou-
> sands of years until the right chemical conditions
> surround and resurrect it, so too are the eternal
> myths passed among us for thousands of generations,
> until the time is ripe for them to flower into life.
>
> Lawrence Blair, *Rhythms of Vision*

HER HEAD IS TILTED TO THE RIGHT. HER GREENISH EYES
are cast downward in an expression of gentle concern.
The mantle that covers her head and shoulders is of a
deep turquoise, studded with gold stars and bordered in
gold. Her hair is black, her complexion olive. She stands
alone, her hands clasped in prayer, an angel at her feet.

She is Our Lady of Guadalupe, a life-sized image of the
Virgin Mary that appeared miraculously on the cactus-
cloth tilma, or cape, of Juan Diego, an Aztec peasant, in
1531, a mere dozen years after Hernán Cortés conquered
Mexico for the King of Spain. For four hundred and fifty
years the colors of the portrait have remained as bright as
if they were painted yesterday. The coarse-woven cactus
cloth, which seldom lasts even twenty years, shows no
signs of decay.

Today Juan Diego's tilma is preserved behind bulletproof glass in a magnificent new basilica in Mexico City, built especially to house the picture. It is placed where pilgrims can view it from as near as twenty-five feet. Yearly, an estimated ten million bow down before the mysterious Virgin, making the Mexico City church the most popular shrine in the Roman Catholic world next to the Vatican.

It is not only Catholics who regard Our Lady of Guadalupe with awe and wonder. The highly respected philosopher F. S. C. Northrop, in *The Meeting of East and West*, wrote that the Image "conveys in some direct and effective way a basic and intuitively felt element in the nature of things and in the heart of human experience." After describing the unending stream of worshippers dropping to the floor at their first sight of the Image, then moving forward on their knees, he said: "Nothing to be seen in Canada or Europe equals it in the volume or the vitality of its moving quality or in the depth of its spirit of religious devotion."

Pope John Paul II, in his address in the Basilica of Our Lady of Guadalupe on January 27, 1979, acknowledged the unwavering appeal of this unique portrait. Addressing the Virgin directly, he said: "When the first missionaries who reached America . . . taught the rudiments of Christian faith, they also taught love for you, the Mother of Jesus and of all people. And ever since the time that the Indian Juan Diego spoke of the sweet Lady of Tepeyac, you, Mother of Guadalupe, have entered decisively into the Christian life of the people of Mexico."

In the 1950s an archaeologist, Father Ostrapovim of

the Russian Orthodox Church, was shown a copy of the painting but was not told of the Image's history or origin. He deduced that the painting was "presumably Eastern-Asiatic, definitely of the Byzantine type." The early Byzantine portraits of the Virgin are believed to approximate her actual appearance most closely. How had such an authentic portrait happened to turn up in Mexico, half a world away?

According to sixteenth-century documents in Nahuatl, the native Aztec language, Juan Diego, his wife, and his uncle had been among the first Aztecs to be converted by the Christian missionaries who had accompanied the Spanish soldiers to Mexico. Juan was fifty years old at the time of his conversion, an advanced age in an era when few lived past forty. A religion that promised redemption and eternal life was far different from the harsh beliefs of the Aztecs, whose gods demanded human sacrifice. When Juan was thirteen he may have witnessed the bloody ceremony dedicating a new temple in nearby Tenochtitlán (Mexico City) in which some eighty thousand captives were put to death.

Juan's wife died two years after her conversion. They had no children and Juan was left alone to take care of his aged uncle, who had been like a father to him. They lived in a hut with a thatched roof and dirt floor. Members of the Aztec servant class, they were among the poorest inhabitants of their small village five miles from Mexico City.

On Saturday, December 9, 1531, Juan Diego left his village before daybreak so he would be in time to hear

Mass celebrated at the church of Santiago in the nearby village of Tlatilolco. On his way, as he passed around the base of a hill called Tepeyac, near which there had once been a shrine to the Aztec mother goddess, he heard a burst of birdsong. At this bleak time of the year, few birds remained, and Juan looked up to see where the song was coming from. On the summit of the hill he saw a bright light.

Suddenly the melodious birdsong ceased, as abruptly as it had begun. From the barren rocks at the top of the hill a voice called him: "Juan! Juanito!"

He climbed the hill quickly and saw on the summit a young woman who seemed to be no more than fourteen years old, standing in a golden mist. She beckoned to him and he knelt before her radiant presence. "Juanito," she said, "the most humble of my sons, where are you going?"

"My Lady," he replied, "I am on my way to church to hear Mass."

"Know then," she continued, "that I am the ever-virgin Holy Mary, Mother of the True God. I wish that a temple be erected here without delay. Go to the bishop's palace in Mexico City, and tell him what I desire."

Assuring her that he would carry out her mission, Juan Diego descended the hill and continued along the road leading to Mexico City.

At the bishop's palace the servants kept him waiting for hours, but at last he was ushered in to the bishop's presence.

Juan de Zumárraga, a Franciscan who was to be formally elected bishop two years later, had come to Mexico in 1528 at the command of the King of Spain, Charles V. He was a powerful but kindly man, who used his influence to lessen the cruelty with which the Spanish soldiers treated the Indians.

He listened sympathetically as his interpreter translated Juan Diego's words from Nahuatl into Spanish, and in reply told Juan Diego to visit him again at some unspecified future date. It was clear to the Indian that he had not been believed.

On his way home, with the sun setting in the west, he climbed once more to the top of Tepeyac and again saw the Virgin Mary. He told her that he had delivered her message but that the bishop did not seem to believe him. He begged her to entrust her mission to someone more important who would be more likely to be believed. But the Virgin insisted that the humble Indian was her chosen messenger. "I command that you go again tomorrow," she said, "and see the bishop. Go in my name, and make known my wish that he has to build a temple here. And again tell him that the ever-virgin Holy Mary, Mother of God, sent you."

Juan Diego promised to follow her instructions and return the following afternoon, at sunset, to give her the bishop's reply.

The next day, a Sunday, Juan again left his home before dawn to go to the village church. It was nearly ten o'clock before the morning services were completed and Juan was able to leave for the bishop's palace. On arriving there, the humble Indian found it even more difficult to be admitted to the bishop's presence. Bishop Zumárraga had not expected the Aztec to return so soon.

This time the bishop questioned Juan Diego more closely. The vivid detail with which the Aztec described his two meetings with the supposedly Heavenly Lady led him to believe that Juan was telling the truth. But perhaps the Indian was deluded. Zumárraga would have been happy to build another church to the honor and glory of the Blessed Virgin, yet if Juan Diego's story was a hoax, the Church could lose a great deal of the ground it had gained with the Indians.

What was needed was proof. He urged Juan to bring a sign from the Heavenly Lady that she had indeed spoken to him, and the bishop would then eagerly comply with her request. Juan agreed without hesitation. As soon as the Indian left, Zumárraga ordered two servants to follow him and report back, but as they neared Tepeyac hill, they lost sight of him. They thought that he had deliberately eluded them, and they reported back to the bishop that he was not to be trusted.

Juan Diego had no idea he was being followed. On the top of the hill he gave the Blessed Virgin the bishop's message, and she told him to return the next day when she would give him the sign the bishop had requested.

That was not to be, because when Juan reached home he found that his uncle was desperately ill. The next day, a Monday, his condition had worsened. The uncle asked Juan to go at daybreak to the village church and bring back a priest to hear his confession, for he was certain he was dying.

Before dawn on Tuesday, Juan Diego went to summon a priest. As he neared Tepeyac hill, he decided to skirt the hill to avoid being detained by any further meeting with the Virgin Mary. But as he rounded the hill, he saw her descending to the plain. He was frightened that he had disappointed her and worried about his uncle, but she reassured him that his uncle would recover and that she was still anxious to provide the bishop with the sign he had requested. She instructed Juan to climb the hill to the same place where he had first seen her and spoken with her, and there to pick some roses and bring them back to her.

Juan climbed the hill with misgivings. It was early December and the barren hilltop was touched with frost. If there had ever been any roses blooming there, they would not be there now.

But when he reached the hilltop he found several varieties of Roses of Castile in full bloom, the petals touched with morning dew. He gathered the roses and put them in his tilma, his loose cape made of two pieces of cactus cloth stitched together. He brought the blossoms to the Virgin and she arranged them in the tilma, saying: "This is the proof and the sign you will take to the bishop. You will tell him in my name that he will see in them my wish and that he will have to comply with it. Rigorously I command you that only before the presence of the bishop will you unfold your mantle and disclose what you are carrying. You will tell him that I ordered you to climb the hilltop, to go and cut the flowers; and all that you saw and admired, so you can induce the prelate to give his support that a temple be built and erected as I have asked."

When he reached the bishop's palace he again had difficulty gaining admittance, until the bishop's servants saw the out-of-season roses peeking from the folds of the tilma. They informed the bishop of the gift the Indian was bringing him, and Zumárraga, guessing that what Juan Diego carried was the proof he had requested, ordered that he be admitted immediately.

When Juan Diego entered, he knelt before the bishop and described his last encounter with "the Lady from Heaven." He then stood and untied his tilma from around his neck so that the roses fell on the floor in a heap. Suddenly, on the cactus cloth of the tilma, there appeared a brightly colored image of the Virgin Mary. The bishop fell to his knees, as did all those present.

The next day Juan Diego took the bishop to the hill where the apparition had appeared and where the Holy Mother had asked that a church be built in her name. The church at Tepeyac was designated the shrine of Our Lady of Guadalupe, in honor of a village in Spain where a small statue of the Virgin had been discovered two hundred years earlier.

News of the miraculous appearance of the Virgin's image on a peasant's cloak spread quickly throughout New Spain. Indians by the thousands, learning that the mother of the Christian God had appeared before one of their own and spoken to him in his native tongue, came from hundreds of miles away to see the image hung above the altar of the new church.

The miraculous picture played a major role in advancing the Church's mission in Mexico. In just seven years, from 1532 to 1538, eight million Indians were converted to Christianity. In one day alone, one thousand couples were married in the sacrament of matrimony.

Throughout the four hundred and fifty years since its first appearance, adoration of the Image of Guadalupe has remained the most striking aspect of Roman Catholic worship in Mexico. Northrop writes of seeing the Image "on the windshield of taxicab after taxicab in Mexico City and in the front interior of almost every bus."

Less pervasive but perhaps more remarkable is the presence of the Image of Guadalupe in churches around the world. Copies of the original or paintings depicting the miracle on the hilltop hang on the walls of churches in Madrid, Rome, Jerusalem, Paris, and even in Taiwan. In the western hemisphere Our Lady of Guadalupe has been crowned in ceremonies in New York City, Newark, New Jersey, and in Cuba, Nicaragua, Uruguay, and Argentina. In every country in Latin America copies of the miraculous picture hang in the churches.

For those millions who come to kneel and pray before the original Image, protected behind bulletproof glass in the new cathedral in Mexico City, Our Lady of Guadalupe with her expression of motherly concern, her olive skin and dark hair, arouses unique feelings of trust and closeness. Many ask for her intercession in heaven to solve their problems on earth, and many return to give thanks when their petitions appear to have been successful.

Tales of the miracles she has wrought abound. In the early seventeenth century, when floods almost destroyed Mexico City, the Image escaped unharmed. In 1921, during the Mexican revolution, a bomb was planted in some flowers placed before the altar of the basilica. The Image hung close behind the altar. Although the bomb exploded, damaging the altar, no one was hurt. Even the glass in front of the picture was unbroken.

Forty years after the Virgin of Guadalupe appeared before Juan Diego she is believed by many to have been responsible for a turning point in Western history. Copies of the Image circulated throughout Europe. Possibly the first and most important of those copies was given to Admiral Giovanni Andrea Doria (grandnephew of the famous Admiral Andrea Doria) by the King of Spain. The young admiral carried the framed picture with him when he took command of a squadron of ships sailing from Genoa to the Gulf of Lepanto (now Corinth) where some three hundred Turkish ships were drawn up, blocking entrance to the gulf. The Christian force, which also numbered some three hundred ships, came around the headland north of the gulf and attempted to meet the Turks head on, but they were outmaneuvered by Turkish forces on the right. Doria's squadron was completely cut off from the rest of the Christian flotilla. At this crucial hour Doria is said to have gone to his cabin, knelt, and prayed to the Image of Guadalupe to save him from certain defeat.

At nightfall, the tide of the sea battle miraculously began to turn. When one Turkish squadron was captured,

the others panicked. Most of the Turkish fleet was destroyed, and fifteen thousand Christians, enslaved in the
Turks' galleys, were freed. The Battle of Lepanto, the last
great naval battle fought under oars, marked the end of
the Ottoman Empire's expansion into the western Mediterranean.

The victory at Lepanto and the thousands of smaller,
less historic miracles imputed to the Virgin of Guadalupe
can be explained in large part as the result of natural
causes. The one miracle that allows of no such natural explanation is that of the Image itself. Why does it show no
sign of cracks or other deterioration after so many years?
Why do the colors remain so bright? Why didn't the
crude fabric on which the Image is imprinted disintegrate long centuries ago?

The search for answers to these and related questions
is the subject of this book.

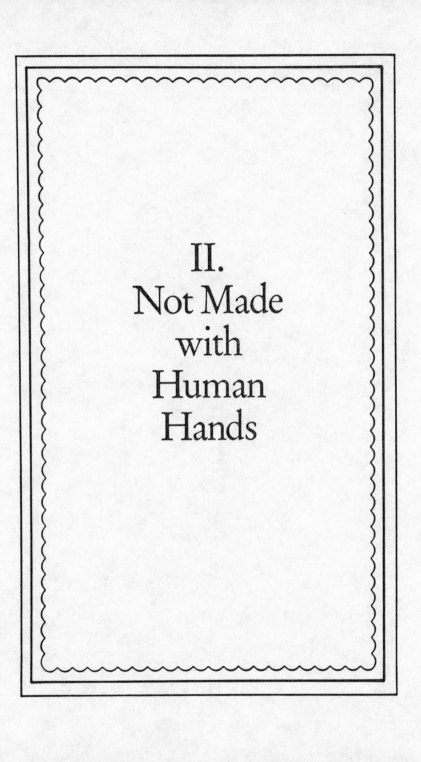

II.
Not Made
with
Human
Hands

> A stone was cut out by no human hands and struck the statue, struck its feet of iron and earthenware and shattered them.
>
> Daniel 2:34

ALTHOUGH I AM NOT A ROMAN CATHOLIC, ON THE MORNING of December 13, 1978, I stood with the throngs outside the Basilica of Guadalupe in Mexico City, waiting to view the Virgin of Guadalupe at first hand. What brought me there was not only the normal curiosity of the tourist but also an understanding of the importance of this famous image, for I am by profession a teacher of philosophy. What exactly was this icon that had had such a powerful effect on men's minds?

Like many millions before me, I was struck by the liveliness of the picture. It seemed to glow, to pulsate, even to breathe.

For those who believe, the explanation is simple. The Image of Guadalupe was made supernaturally. No artist painted it. It was not made with human hands.

There is a long tradition in the Church of belief in creation without human intervention, beginning with the virgin birth of Jesus. Indeed, as was pointed out by Saint

Irenaeus, an early Christian writer of the second century A.D., the Virgin Mary can be considered the mother of all things created supernaturally.

The first work of art that was said to be "not made with hands" (the Greek word is *acheiropoietos*) was a portrait of Christ, discovered around the year 550 in Edessa (now Urfa, Turkey). It came to be known as the "Image of Edessa" or the Mandylion. In the tenth century it was taken to Constantinople. Three hundred years later, during the Fourth Crusade, it disappeared.

Artists' copies of the Mandylion made before its disappearance show a blurred image of Christ's head ranging from sepia to rust-brown. The color, writes Ian Wilson in *The Shroud of Turin*, is "virtually identical to the coloring of the image on the Shroud." Some people believe that the Mandylion and the Shroud of Turin are one and the same, which Wilson strongly supports, by virtue of his own theory that the Shroud was *folded*, then tucked away in a frame with only the upper part visible.

The two images of Christ belong unquestionably with that group of objects believed to have been created supernaturally. They bring to mind the fabled portrait of Christ named "Veronica's Veil." According to medieval legend, a woman named Veronica gave Christ a cloth to wipe the sweat from his face while he was on the road to Calvary. The imprint of his face was left on the cloth.

Buddhist tradition describes a similar imprint made by the Buddha on a cloth. Such a tradition, of ascribing a supernatural source for objects of veneration, including portraits of religious figures, is an ancient one.

Whatever the power of such objects to answer man's spiritual needs, in recent years there has been a widespread effort to establish their authenticity by the use of new scientific techniques of dating and chemical analysis. At the time I first viewed the Image of Guadalupe, the Shroud of Turin was front-page news throughout the Western world as a result of research by teams of European and American scientists. One of the scientists appeared to have established beyond question that the Shroud originated in the eastern Mediterranean, in Turkey or Palestine, in the first century A.D., although the Shroud's documented history went no further back than the fourteenth century in France and Italy.

I could not help but wonder what sort of light scientific research would shed on the Image of Guadalupe. The Guadalupan Image and the Turin Shroud are, of course, very different. The image said to be Christ on the Shroud is faint and shadowy and in one color only, while the Image of Guadalupe is vivid and lifelike, with several bright colors. Clearly a different technique produced each image, but the scientific methods being used to authenticate the Shroud might apply equally well to Guadalupe.

Efforts to confirm or repudiate the supernatural origin of the Image of Guadalupe are not new. As long ago as 1556, twenty-five years after Juan Diego untied his tilma in Bishop Zumárraga's palace, a formal investigation was launched by the Church authorities. The investigation appears to have been an outgrowth of rivalries between the Dominican and Franciscan brotherhoods and their di-

vergent understanding of what constituted a proper form
of worship for the millions of new Indian converts.

In a sworn statement representing the views of Francisco de Bustamante, a provincial priest, a representative
of the Franciscan viewpoint named Juan de Maseques reported that Bustamante

> and all the other religious had tried with great insistence
> that the natives of this land did not have their devotions
> and prayers represented in painting or sculpture, in order
> to prevent them from exercising their old rites and
> ceremonies to their idols, and that this new devotion to
> Our Lady of Guadalupe seems to be an opportunity to
> return to the practices which they previously had . . .

The shrine which held the Image of Guadalupe had been
erected on a hill directly in front of the spot where there
had been an important temple dedicated to the Aztec virgin goddess Tonantzin, "Little Mother" of the Earth and
Corn. Tonantzin had been one of the most popular
figures in the Aztec pantheon of gods and goddesses. So
Bustamante's concern that the Aztecs, by their adoration
of the Image of Guadalupe, might be reverting to their
pagan beliefs, was soundly based. Another priest, Alonso
de Santiago, testified that

> the aforementioned Fray Francisco de Bustamante said
> . . . that seeing the multitude of people that go there be-
> cause of the fame of that image, painted yesteryear by an
> Indian, performing miracles was again undoing what
> previously had been done.

De Maseques went on to supply the name of the reputed artist, saying that the Image "was a painting that the Indian painter Marcos had done."

There was an artist of that name active in Mexico around that time. But why didn't Marcos Cipac, as he was known, simply attend the formal investigation and put the matter to rest? It is unlikely that he could have been bribed to stay away, for any deceit involving the Holy Mother of God would have been dangerous for a Spaniard, let alone an Aztec. If Marcos was already dead, a fellow artist could easily have come in his place to present testimony, just as Bustamante's testimony was presented by De Maseques.

In the investigation of 1556, no mention is made of Juan Diego and the legend of the Virgin's three appearances before him. Was the omission deliberate, or in the intervening twenty-five years had the effort to exterminate Indian idol worship also extended to the legend of a miracle involving an Indian peasant?

The other side of the controversy was represented by a member of the Dominican order, Alonso de Montufar, who replaced Zumárraga as Archbishop of New Spain. On September 8, 1556, some weeks before the formal investigation and on a date widely regarded as the birthday of the Virgin Mary, Archbishop Montufar preached a sermon in the small church on Tepeyac hill. Standing in front of the Image of Guadalupe, he asked that the Image be accorded special status as an object of worship. He meant by this to exempt the Image from the ban on icons then being enforced throughout New Spain in an effort to stamp out whatever remained of Aztec idol worship.

A world-renowned scholar of the Nahuatl language, Ángel M. Garibay-Kintana, discovered Montufar's sermon in the mid-1940s and published it in 1955 and 1961 in Spanish and English translations. In his comments on the sermon, Garibay calls attention to an unusual alteration in the order of service of the Mass celebrated at Tepeyac:

> In the sermons of that epoch it was customary to take as the text for the day of the Nativity of the Virgin the Gospel . . . which was and still is the genealogy of Christ given in the first chapter of Saint Matthew. The text is "Mary, of whom Jesus was born, who is called the Christ." We have hundreds of sermons in our libraries which take these words as the basis for the explanation of the dignity and offices of Mary in the work of redemption. On this occasion Archbishop Montufar broke that tradition, quoting Saint Luke in the text: "Blessed are the eyes which see what you see."

The substitution of this passage from Luke for the traditional first chapter of Matthew, says Garibay, "gives us a clue by which we can penetrate the mind of the prelate. Our Lord congratulates the Apostles because they are seeing something new . . . new and extraordinary, not to be confounded with any other deeds . . . the presence on earth of the Son of God made flesh." Thus, Garibay concludes, "If Archbishop Montufar, who was a good theologian and a strict Thomist, took the liberty on this occasion of applying these words to Mary and to her Image, it was because he saw something in it that could not be found in any other images. He believed, twenty-five years after the event, that he had found something truly extraordinary."

In the years following his sermon at Tepeyac, Archbishop Montufar authorized construction of a considerably larger building there, replacing the tiny chapel in which he conducted the Mass in 1556. The new church was completed some time before the end of 1567, according to the best-known historian of that period, Bernardino de Sahagún. Sahagún, a Franciscan, was not enthusiastic about the Virgin of Guadalupe. He complained, with some reason, that certain priests insulted the Virgin Mary by referring to her by the Nahuatl name of Tonantzin, the name of the Aztec goddess, which means, literally, "Our Mother." Sahagún thought that the term for the Virgin Mary in Nahuatl should be "Dios-nantzin," meaning "God's Mother."

In 1570 Montufar sent to King Philip II of Spain an oil-painted copy of the Image of Guadalupe. Archbishop Montufar had commissioned the painting from an artist who remains unidentified. The fact that Montufar sent a copy of the Image to the king of the world's then most powerful nation proves that, despite the controversy surrounding the Image, it was indeed being venerated by many.

This copy of the Image is believed to be the one Admiral Doria carried aboard ship during the Battle of Lepanto in 1571. The portrait was given by a cardinal of the

Doria family to the Church of Santo Stefano in Aveto, Italy, where it remains to this day.

In recent years, scholars have brought to light several sixteenth-century documents which confirm that there was widespread belief in the miraculous appearance of the Virgin on Tepeyac hill. Most of these documents now lie in the Mexican National Library, in the library of the Basilica of Guadalupe, or in museums and libraries in New York and Paris. Among the most impressive of these documents are four Aztec *anales*, or yearbooks, discovered by two twentieth-century Mexican priests, Mariano Cuevas and Bravo Ugarte. Here are some representative selections referring to the Image of Guadalupe:

(A)

5 tecpatl, 1510: in this new year came a president to Mexico; in the same year arrived first a prelate of the status of bishop, his name Fray Francisco de Zumárraga, of the religious order of Saint Francis; and then appeared Our Beloved Mother of Guadalupe.

(B)

1510 tecpatl: then came a new president to Mexico, governor; in the same year, Our Beloved Mother of Guadalupe appeared and manifested Herself to the poor Indian named Juan Diego.

(C)

In the year of 1555, Saint Mary made herself to appear on Tepeyac.

(D)

    13 acatl, 1531: the Castilians founded Cuitlaxcoapan, Puebla de los Angeles, and to Juan Diego was manifested the Beloved Lady of Guadalupe in Mexico, that is named Tepeyac.

The inconsistency in dating is explained by the difficulty in reconciling the Aztec and European calendars. Furthermore, the Nahuatl language used picture symbols rather than letters or numbers. According to historian Ugarte, the authors of these sixteenth-century annals no more knew "how to write arabic numerals, much less how to form a running enumeration" than how to write a letter, word, or sentence in Latin-lettered Spanish.

If we check the annals against actual events, we find that "1510" is probably 1528, for that is the year Zumárrage is known to have arrived in Mexico. The second *anale* may refer to 1530, the year that the Spanish king, in response to a plea from Zumárraga to put an end to the cruel treatment of the Indians, sent a second administrator to New Spain. This would correspond with the mention of a "new president, new governor." But none of these annals were written at the time of the Virgin's apparition. They were recorded a decade or more after the event, so the actual dates could well have become blurred by the passage of time.

    Further corroboration exists, however. One is a description of the Guadalupan shrine written by Suárez de Peralta, a Spaniard who retired to Spain in 1570. The shrine, he reports, "contained . . . a very holy Image which . . . has performed many miracles. She appeared among the rocks, and the whole country is devoted to her."

Another historical confirmation of the Image's supernatural origin was made by Francisco Verdugo Quetzalmalitzín. In 1558, only two years after Montufar's sermon in the Tepeyac chapel, Quetzalmalitzín made a collection of documents in Nahuatl that directly referred to the Guadalupan apparition and Image. That collection of documents has now disappeared but reference to it is made in the famous Boturini Collection.

The most complete and most famous source for the legend of Juan Diego is a document written in the sixteenth century by an Indian named Antonio Valeriano. For many years the document was considered a seventeenth-century fraud, because of doubts concerning the actual existence of the reputed author. Until independent proof of Valeriano's existence could be located, the question remained insoluble. But a few years ago, from an archive in the library of the Mexican National University, there came to light a sixteenth-century civil paper with the clear signature, Antonio Valeriano, at its bottom.

Valeriano's story of Juan Diego is called the *nican mopohua* (literally "an account") and is given in full in the Appendices. A dating device in common use among historians places the document as being written sometime between 1540 and 1580. That device is handwriting style, which changes from period to period in all cultures, often in only a few decades. By comparing the penmanship of documents we know were written in the sixteenth century with the penmanship of the *nican mopohua* we can confirm that it too is a product of the sixteenth century.

Another sixteenth-century document, known merely as the "Primitive Relation," was unearthed from the Mexican National Library Archives. Nahuatl scholar Garibay appears to have found it first. With the incorporation of the Center for Guadalupan Studies in Mexico City in 1976, this important work received further scholarly attention by Father Mario Rojas, leading to wider recognition of its value in authenticating the origin of the Image of Guadalupe.

The Primitive Relation, which also appears in full in the Appendices, was probably written about 1573 by the historian Juan de Tovar, who transcribed the story from a still-earlier source. Garibay believes that the earlier source was Juan González, who is thought to have been Bishop Zumárraga's translator in 1531.

The thirty-nine short paragraphs of the Primitive Relation begin with these words: "This is the great marvel that Our Lord made through the medium of the always-virgin Saint Mary." One of the two direct quotations in the text ascribed to the apparition of the Virgin Mary gives a direct clue to the time when the Primitive Relation was written. The apparition, addressing Juan Diego, says:

> My little son, walk to the center of the great City of Mexico. Say there to the Spiritual Governor, the Archbishop, that here in Tepeyac they make me a habitation, they raise me a little house, so that the faithful Christians can

come pray to me. There in it I will convert, when they make me their counsel.

The Primitive Relation had to be written down sometime *after* Zumárraga became the Archbishop of Mexico.

A final sixteenth-century source documenting the miracle on Tepeyac was found in Peru in 1924 by M. H. Saville, an anthropologist. It is a pictorial calendar, known as the Codex Saville or the Codex Tetlapalco (from the city where it was found). It now rests in the collection of the Museum of the American Indian in New York City.

The Saville-Tetlapalco Codex records Aztec history from the year 1430 to 1557. Discs on the calendar were used by the Indians to signify the passage of time. Mariano Cuevas, who translated the calendar in 1929 (his translation appears in the Appendices), gives the following comments regarding a female figure located next to the top of the disc representing the year 1531:

> A virgin with her hands folded near her heart; her head bent toward her right shoulder, dressed in a salmon-colored tunic and a greenish blue mantilla—see the unique design as in the original—is the Virgin of Guadalupe as venerated at Tepeyac, four miles north of Mexico City, and some six miles south of San Marcos. By painting it a little lower than the year 1532, it is well indicated that her year was 1531.

Given this historical evidence, much of which has come to light only recently, there seems little reason to doubt that the Image of Guadalupe was a recognized object of worship in the sixteenth century, beginning in 1531 or soon thereafter.

A second official inquiry concerning the Image of Guadalupe was conducted by the Church authorities in 1666, one hundred and ten years after the first. The first part of the inquiry consisted of testimony from the oldest Aztecs still alive regarding their memories of the origin of the painting. They were unanimous in maintaining that there had been an apparition of the Virgin Mary and that she had made the miraculous Image. After the Indians, several artists and scientists were called on to testify. Was there indeed anything unusual, perhaps supernatural, about this painting of Mary?

Nineteen years earlier, in 1647, the Image had been covered with glass for the first time. The Image was taken down from the wall, the glass cover removed, and master artist Juan Salguero and his associates were given one hour to examine the painting.

The artists were truly surprised by what they saw. As had been rumored, the picture was painted not on canvas but on an Aztec tilma. The artists could clearly see the vertical seam running down the middle of the cloak, which must have made the painting of a portrait even more difficult. The tilma was made of roughly woven cactus cloth, which was known to disintegrate in only a few years. Salguero concluded that this tendency to rapid disintegration should, if anything, have been hastened by the fact that the paints had been applied directly to the bare, burlap-like surface. The cactus cloth had not been sized or prepared in any way. It had not been stretched to provide a firm surface for the painter, as a canvas would have been, and there was no filler in the holes between the loosely woven fibers.

The artists on that March day in 1666 were genuinely perplexed. Not only should paint applied to an unprepared surface—any surface, and certainly the inferior cactus cloth—have rotted it within a few years, but how had the artist contrived to paint such a beautiful human face on so rough a cloth?

And what about the colors of the painting? Could they be paints, and if so, what kind of pigments could be made to adhere to such a rough, unprepared surface? Futhermore, these paints—if they were paints—were not faded or browned, nor were they cracked or peeling. In a painting more than a hundred years old, this was unimaginable.

Of the many mysterious aspects of the Image, none was more of a puzzle than the apparent mixing of media. Salguero and his fellow artists saw at once that the coloring material used for the portrait was of several different types. How had watercolor and oil, if that was what they were, been blended so perfectly into each other?

The artists concluded, in sworn testimony, that

> . . . it is impossible for any human craftsman to paint or create a work so fine, clean, and well-formed on a fabric so coarse as this tilma or ayate, on which this divine and sovereign painting of the Most Holy Virgin, Our Lady of Guadalupe, is painted.

Fifteen days later, on March 28, the Physicians Royal came to examine the painting. They were particularly struck by its remarkable state of preservation, not only regarding the colors and the untreated cactus cloth, but also because of another factor, which should have destroyed the painting long ago—namely, the high concentration of niter or saltpeter in the humid air. The church was situated next to a large lake, Texcoco, which was known to contain the caustic chemical. Moisture-laden breezes off the water carried the chemical into the atmosphere, and caused serious damage to another noted painting which hung in a nearby church.

The Physicians Royal also made a close examination of the back of the tilma—and they were probably the last to do so. A few years later the tilma was permanently backed by a half-inch-thick plate of silver.

The back of the tilma provided another source of astonishment, for on the back was an oval patch of green, a color that was nowhere to be seen on the front. One observer described the color as comparable to "the leaves of lilies."

The scientific observers noted still another odd property of the picture. When the tilma was held up to the light, it was so thin they could see right through it. As explained in their testimony, this did not mean that they saw through the holes in the loosely woven cloth but rather literally *through* the translucent fibers themselves. What was even stranger, the green on the back could not be seen from the front, although the Image of the Virgin was clearly perceived from the back. The Physicians Royal commented:

> The understanding wavers, discourse confuses, and the prodigy refers itself to the realm of mystery, as Aristotle, prince of philosophers, asserts an incontrovertible principle: *Idem in quantum idem, semper est natum facere idem* (The same element in the same matter, with the same arrangement, can only produce the same effect). Why does the color green, which this tilma bears on its opposite side, not pass through at all to the front side? God alone, Who made it, knows why.

The inquiry of 1666 came in response to the widening fame of the Image of Guadalupe. Acceptance of the image as divinely created—"not with human hands"—had been growing, primarily because of the writings of two priests. The first, Miguel Sánchez, in 1648 published in Mexico City in Spanish a work entitled *Image of the Virgin Mary, Guadalupan Mother of God*, a theological discussion of the story of the apparition and the creation of the Image. The following year a fellow priest named Lasso de Vega published the *Huey Tlanahuicoltica* which told the story of the miraculous painting in the Indians' native language, Nahuatl. Vega, in his preface, insisted that he was presenting an edited version of the story as it appeared in earlier Nahuatl sources (probably the *nican mopohua* mentioned above and given in full in the Appendices), but many skeptics accused him of merely producing a popular, Indian-language edition of Sánchez's book. Slowly, that view has changed, and now it is generally believed that Vega did in fact use earlier Nahuatl sources for his book. Yet largely because of the apparent hundred-year delay in publishing the story of the Image of Guadalupe, many thoughtful people throughout the years had come to regard the entire narrative as no more than an interesting fable.

The next extensive study of the Image was made about a hundred years later by the famous painter Miguel Cabrera. Cabrera's book *American Marvel* appeared in 1756. In it he confirmed everything that had been observed by the 1666 specialists, and was equally at a loss to explain how the painting had been produced or why it had endured so remarkably well. He noted that the cactus cloth was indeed without sizing and that the only other material present in the picture was a more-expensive cotton thread used to sew the two vertical panels of the tilma together. In chapter six of his book he marvels at the gold powder used for the stars on the Virgin's blue mantle, since gold powder was unknown to artists of the sixteenth century.

In chapters five and seven Cabrera undertakes to answer objections raised against the reputed miracle. Is the figure of the Virgin off-center? Of course, in order to avoid the vertical seam of the tilma. Isn't one leg shorter than the other? Yes, to capture ingeniously the Virgin's slight bow. Aren't the hands too small in relation to the overall figure? At first look it seems so, Cabrera admits, but a closer study shows that such delicate hands are typical of ladies of all countries.

Cabrera also noted the surprising mixture of media in

the Image. "I find it . . . extraordinary," he writes, "that in a painting there are together on one surface four distinct species of media such as we find miraculously united in . . . Our Lady of Guadalupe. The science of aesthetics can deal with each of these media separately, but there is no authority . . . who can adequately treat of their coming together on one canvas . . . Specifically the head and hands were executed in oils; the tunic . . . angel and clouds . . . in tempera; mantle . . . watercolor; the background, a fresco.

"Oil painting," Cabrera explains, "is executed in oleaginous pigments which when dry blend and attain harmony only when the surface of the canvas is properly prepared by sizing—then this is the most marvelous medium available. The second, tempera, employs pigments of all colors with gum, glue, or similar bases. The third, watercolor, is executed on fine, white material and necessitates soaking the obverse side of the surface so that the whole is permeated with color. Fresco painting, the fourth medium, is a plastering and coloring of the surface in the same action . . . it requires a firm, solid surface such as a board, stone, etc. . . . each in itself demands . . . a peculiar mastery of technique . . ."

Concluding, Cabrera says that "the most talented and careful painter if he set himself to copy this sacred Image on a canvas of this poor quality, without using sizing, and attempting to imitate the four media employed, would at last, after great and wearisome travail, admit that he had not succeeded."

The portrait artist speaks from not only his own experience, but also that of his contemporaries: " . . . this can be clearly verified in the numerous copies that have been made with the benefit of varnish, on the most carefully prepared canvases, and using only one medium, oil, which offers the greatest facility . . . there has not been one which is a perfect reproduction—as the best, placed beside the original, clearly shows."

About three decades later, José Ignacio Bartolache, a skeptical physician who was also a priest, insisted on retesting Cabrera's thesis. In 1789 he ordered eleven copies made of the painting. Procuring the services of the best artists in Mexico, he insisted that each utilize only color agents which were known to have been in use in the sixteenth century. For example, for the color red he would allow only mercuric oxide or sulfate, or a vegetable dye from the "dragon's-blood flower," or plants such as the "ruby," the "brazil-red," and the sunflower.

What were the results of Bartolache's experiment? All reproductions had been painted on cactus cloth of the same inferior type as the original, and in 1796, seven years later, all eleven copies still survived. Clearly something in the pigments used had preserved the crude material. Perhaps the mystery of the cactus cloth was solved. How, then, to explain that, while all the copies had survived, one was in such a poor state, peeling and coated with fungus, that it had to be removed from public display. This copy was the one which had been placed beside the original at the Basilica of Guadalupe on Tepeyac hill.

Studies made of the Image since Bartolache's time

have yielded similar results. Since 1950, two artists, Francisco Campa Rivera and Francisco de Guadalupe Mojica, have examined the painting. Their reports are in the Basilica Archives. Rivera, who came to Mexico from Barcelona in 1941, studied the painting in 1954 and 1963.

Like Bartolache, Rivera was interested in the media used. In addition to attempting to make copies using oils, watercolors, and tempera, he experimented with pastels and inks of various colors. Whatever media he used, the color could be seen on both sides of the cactus cloth, which was not true of the green patch on the back of the original. Nor was Rivera able satisfactorily to determine the composition of the original colors of the painting.

Rivera and Mojica agreed that by the mid-1950s a number of additions had been made to the painting. When these had occurred they were unable to tell, but none of the alterations affected significant areas of the Image. They involved such things as the black outlining of dress and mantle and restoration of the gold rays around the entire figure. The angel and crescent at the Virgin's feet were also believed to be additions, as were the fleur-de-lis on the robe, since if they had been part of the initial painting they would have been shown as falling between its folds.

Mojica is convinced of the miraculous nature of the Image. Because of many details—for example, the robe, which is of the same style as that worn by ancient Palestinian women—he believes the Image is an authentic portrait of the Virgin. Rivera, an established critic as well as an artist, began with the hypothesis that the work was anonymously done by a European master or by a Mexican strongly under European influence. He reluctantly abandoned this view when he was unable to identify any Spanish, Flemish, or Italian characteristics in the painting.

In addition to Marcos Cipac, mentioned in the inquiry of 1556, two other Aztec artists known to have been active in the sixteenth century have been suggested as possible creators of the painting. Their names are Pedro Chachalaca and Francisco Xinmamal. But they are, ultimately, only names. We have less reason to associate them with the picture than we do Cipac.

Over the centuries, there have been repeated attempts to disprove the miraculous origin of the Image of Guadalupe. Most frequently cited are the comments of a famous nineteenth-century Mexican historian, Joaquín García Icazbalceta, in his introduction to a new edition of the official inquiry of 1556. He chose to interpret several key phrases of that inquiry as indicating that veneration of the Image of Guadalupe merely echoed the earlier worship of Aztec idols, and that the legend of Juan Diego and the apparition of the Virgin was a later invention. The fact that the 1556 inquiry made no mention of the apparition is taken as proof by Icazbalceta and by twentieth-century historian Jacques LaFaye that the story had not existed at that time.

Both Icazbalceta and LaFaye cite a section of the inquiry in which the delegate, speaking for the Franciscan Bustamante, mentions the shrine at Loreto, Italy. Loreto has been revered as a shrine to the Virgin Mary since medieval times. LaFaye believes that Bustamante would, on mentioning Loreto, have gone on to compare it with Tepeyac, if the apparition story had been known in his day.

This seems reasonable enough, but I believe the inquiry's silence about the apparition at Tepeyac was deliberate. It is equally feasible that Bustamante's reference to Loreto was an indirect way of disputing the Tepeyac story. The point is not that the Loreto shrine was the site of an apparition, but that it was the site of an *approved* apparition. In fact, in the 1556 inquiry, Bustamante explicitly notes the sound basis on which the Church awarded official sanction to the Loreto shrine. The Franciscan's dilemma was not, I think, whether to endorse one and not the other; it was to decide whether or not to endorse both.

Like many people, I share some of Bustamante's skepticism. But, while he had no qualms about accepting the existence of an apparition at Loreto and the reality of the supernatural in general, today most of us shy away from the very idea of the supernatural, though we have a most imperfect notion of what it might be.

Recent scholarship, especially among the Indian Archives of the the Mexican National Library, has brought to light several documents which, if they do not prove the actuality of the Virgin's supernatural appearance before an Indian peasant in 1531, do at least confirm the fact that belief in that appearance was widespread in those times. No historiographical technique can irrefutably prove that any past event did in fact occur, be it mundane or supernatural. The historian can locate, collate, and compare materials relevant to a disputed question, but there his own special expertise ends.

However, in the case of the Virgin of Guadalupe, the Image itself survives. As my researches drew me deeper and deeper into the subject, I became convinced that first-hand scientific examination of the painting would enable us to transcend the limitations of the historian.

III.
Impossible Coincidences

> Synchronicity . . . means the simultaneous occur-
> rence of a certain psychic state with one or more ex-
> ternal events which appear as meaningful parallels
> to the momentary subjective state—and, in certain
> cases, vice versa.
>
> Carl Gustav Jung,
> *The Structure and Dynamics of the Psyche*

THE SCIENTIFIC FINDINGS REGARDING THE SHROUD OF TURIN were very much on my mind as I flew back from Mexico City to my home in Florida. I considered it a good omen when I picked up the candy on my dinner tray and found printed on the wrapper "Made in Turin, Italy."

Following my first visit to the Basilica of Guadalupe in December 1978, I had arranged a meeting with an associate of the abbot of the basilica, Monseñor Enrique Salazar, to discuss the possibility of subjecting the Image of Guadalupe to scientific study. Immediately after my meeting with the monseñor, I met with Abbot D. Guillermo Schulenburg-Prado. He and Monseñor Salazar assured me that, if I could satisfy certain requirements, they would permit the famous tilma to be removed from its frame and protective glass. However, this could not be arranged until sometime after Pope John Paul II's visit to Mexico, scheduled for January 1979.

What I had specifically proposed was that the Image be subjected to such techniques as computer enhancement and infrared photography. The last time the glass cover had been removed for photography was in 1961 when official color prints of the portrait had been made. Only one infrared photograph of the Image had ever been taken—by Jesús Catano in March 1946—and great strides had been made since then in the techniques of infrared photography.

Feeling that I had at least tentative approval from the Church authorities, on returning to Florida I proceeded at once to try to locate a scientist with special expertise in the field of biophysics, someone who could direct the research and interpret the results. Among many possibilities, Dr. Philip Serna Callahan had come to my attention through his study of Unidentified Flying Objects. An entomologist with a background in biophysics, Dr. Callahan had advanced the hypothesis that, in certain cases at least, UFOs were atmospherically lighted insect swarms.

After several weeks spent trying to locate him, I discovered that he also lived in Florida. As I dialed the phone to speak with him, I felt a natural anxiety. I had no reason to suppose that Dr. Callahan would have any interest at all in a religious object hanging on the wall of a church in Mexico City.

But, after I briefly described the Image and the research that I proposed be done, Dr. Callahan told me of his interest in the Shroud of Turin. He was soon to present his conclusions in a lecture. From his enthusiasm I knew at once that he was the man I was looking for, and I arranged to visit him within the week.

Although he had given me directions for finding his house, dusk had already fallen on that day in late January 1979, but I had not yet arrived at his door. My thoughts drifted back to another appointment, a few weeks earlier: I had huddled off the bridge spanning the Pascagoula River, stung by the freezing wind, the hurtling rush-hour traffic darting by in the darkness. I was looking for an interesting individual, but I had no thoughts of Guadalupe.

He had an unlisted telephone, so I went to the local police station for help. All seemed lost until the county constable, overhearing my dilemma, stepped out of an adjoining office and personally located my "appointment." As I left the police station I saw a church across the street. Looking up, I noted a shimmering golden disc inside of which was painted a large picture of the Virgin Mary. The name of the church was Our Lady of the Victories. Several months later I uncovered the fact, already related here, that a copy of the Image of Guadalupe had been on board Doria's flagship during the Battle of Lepanto. The Christians' triumph in that battle led Saint Pius V to name the day, October 7, 1571, "Our Lady of Victory."

It had been a good omen, for my interview with Dr. Callahan that evening was everything I hoped it would be. Together we mapped out detailed plans for research with two specific objectives in mind—one, to discover whether there was an undersketch beneath the picture, because if such an undersketch existed, the Image was undoubtedly the work of a human artist; and two, to determine the composition of the coloring materials used.

Infrared photography of old or possibly valuable paintings is today a routine procedure, of immeasurable help in determining the age and authenticity of the paintings. Pigments used by artists in bygone times were quite different from those in use since the late nineteenth century, when aniline dyes were first introduced. Aniline-derived pigments when seen under infrared light are radically dissimilar from earlier pigments, although the difference cannot be seen in ordinary light.

Throughout my dealings with the Church authorities, which occupied my time in the early months of 1979, I kept in constant touch with Dr. Callahan, informing him of the progress of our negotiations. I did not learn until months afterward that at one point, on reviewing his numerous previous commitments and after a bout with flu, he had seriously considered bowing out of the Guadalupe investigation.

What changed his mind was something he unearthed one evening while reading his family history. Callahan's Irish father had married a Mexican woman whose ancestry traced back several hundred years. On that night Dr. Callahan first learned that a direct ancestor had been one of the group of missionaries and explorers who set out from Mexico for the sparsely settled northern territory known as California. At the end of their journey they founded the city of San Francisco, but before leaving the vicinity of Mexico City they had stopped at a shrine to pray for the success of their mission. The shrine was the Church of Our Lady of Guadalupe on Mount Tepeyac.

How account for the fact that out of the scores of scientists I considered, the one I chose to help me in the Guadalupe project was one whose ancestor had clearly accepted the supernatural origin of the Image?

Now, however, it was our task to assure the Church authorities that no harm would come to the painting as a result of our proposed examination. I wrote to Mrs. Georgina López-Freixes, assistant to the abbot of the basilica, in January, requesting copies of certain documents in the basilica library, which she sent me without delay. Throughout, Dr. Callahan and I were helped immeasurably by Mrs. López, by the abbot, Dr. Schulenburg-Prado, and by the basilica's executive, Monseñor Enrique Salazar. Later, Father Luis Medina, president of the Center for Guadalupan Studies, and Father Maurilio Montemayor, secretary of the Center, gave us invaluable assistance.

Pope John Paul II visited the basilica on January 27, 1979. Shortly after his unprecedented visit, the abbot and Monseñor Salazar informed us that sometime in the spring the sacred Image would be taken down and the glass and frames removed so we could take the proposed series of infrared photographs and black and white close-ups suitable for computer enhancement.

Our excitement grew. What would we find? Would the infrared photos reveal an undersketch? Would closeup examination show signs of retouching, which would explain the unfading brightness of the colors? Had some

kind of sizing or preservative been applied to the coarse
cactus cloth?

These questions coursed through my mind day after
day as I waited for a definite date to be set.

Yet my mind was not inactive. Particularly not my sub-
conscious self, if Arthur Koestler's theories of "coincidence" or synchronicity are at all valid.

I had been reading voluminously. I began to believe
that the Mexican history of the Guadalupe, although
highly significant, was not the entire story. Research im-
plied a continental base, or something even further east;
in any event, far earlier. About this time, these intuitions
were confirmed in reading a history by Jacques Lafaye,
who proposed a strong case linking the Mexican Madonna
with an almost identically named Spanish image, Our
Lady of Guadalupe of Estremadura. I remember that I
skimmed over that point. In fact, I half wished to forget
such a manifest complication. It dropped out of memory.

Then a television reporter called to interview me. Asked
directions to my recently purchased home, I gave him the
reference of a park, across the tree-lined street. As this
park had no posted name, I was surprised to hear him
speak of one. He had found the title on his wall-sized
map. But I made no association, turning instead to the
matter of the imminent interview.

Several hours later, as I was about to retire, I remembered all of a sudden the name of the park across the
street. It was Estremadura!

I did not go immediately to sleep that night.

IV.
In
Search
of
Mary

Lycomedes! What meanest thou by this matter of a portrait? Can it be one of thy gods which is painted here? I see that thou art still living in a heathen fashion.

Apocryphal Acts of John

ONCE THE DETAILS OF OUR PROJECT RECEIVED OFFICIAL APproval, I could return to my historical research. I was particularly eager to discover whether any portrait of Mary from life had ever been made. If such a portrait existed, and if the Image of Guadalupe had truly been created without human intervention, the two pictures should resemble each other.

Many people believe erroneously that widespread veneration of the Virgin Mary did not begin until the late Middle Ages, when magnificent churches such as the cathedral at Chartres were built in her name. But the date accepted by most scholars as the beginning of veneration for the Holy Mother is the Council of Ephesus, A.D. 431. Even earlier, in A.D. 245, the philosopher Origen termed Mary *Theotókos*, meaning Mother of God. And beneath the new Roman Catholic Church of the Annunciation in Nazareth archaeologists have found "Hail Mary" scrawled in Greek on walls dating back to the second century.

Although this evidence of extremely early veneration of Mary is tantalizing, it provides no assurance that an authentic portrait of the Virgin ever existed. There is generally believed to have been a prohibition among the earliest Christians against all religious art, whether painting or sculpture. In the early fifth century Saint Augustine of Hippo wrote: "As to Christ and His Mother, we know nothing of their true appearance."

Despite Saint Augustine's blunt statement, evidence to the contrary exists. Around A.D. 326, Eusebius of Caesarea, a confidant of Constantine the Great, wrote the first comprehensive ecclesiastical history. In that history Eusebius says that not only had there apparently been religious art in the first century of Christianity, but that statues and paintings of Christ Himself had been made:

> They say that the statue is a portrait of Jesus . . . nor is it strange that those of the Gentiles who, of old, were benefited by our Savior, should have done such things, since we have already learned that the likenesses of Peter and Paul, and of Christ Himself, *are preserved in paintings,* the ancients being accustomed, as it is likely according to the habits of the Gentiles, to pay this kind of honor indiscriminately to those regarded by them as deliverers. (italics added)

Eusebius himself may have seen the statue he refers to, for others report seeing such a statue in a church at Paneas, in Palestine. The statue was said to show Christ healing the woman with the blood disease, as recounted in the Gospels.

Eusebius further mentions paintings of Peter and Paul. Coin-sized medallions of these saints continue to be found in Rome even today. From the style of composition and manufacture, we know that they date from before 325.

André Grabar, a historian of Christian art, believes that both the medallions and the Paneas statue are of no later than second-century origin. "However astonishing it may seem," he observes, "these images appear at a period which has left us no equivalent images of Christ. Is this a matter of chance? Or is it, rather, that the monuments that have been preserved testify to the actuality? In the latter event, the monuments would be of considerable moment (corresponding to a first blaze of Christian portraiture, afterwards extinguished). They would be comparable to written testimony on Christian portraits from the beginning of our era."

Grabar's suggestion that the early Christians made portraits of the Church fathers and Christ, soon thereafter lost or destroyed in the wave of iconoclasm that swept Christianity in the eighth and ninth centuries, allows us to entertain the possibility that there may, after all, have been an authentic portrait of the Virgin Mary.

Generally accepted as the earliest Madonna is a crude painting, found in the Catacombs of Priscilla in Rome. Usually dated from the late second century, it gives us little idea of Mary's appearance.

More interesting is an ancient legend brought to light in 1887 by Christian historian Ferdinand Gregorovius. The legend may well contain more than an atom of truth.

As Saint Luke lay dying in the Greek city of Thebes, he revealed that for years he had carried with him a genuine portrait of Christ's Mother. He asked his disciple Ananias to take care of the portrait after his death.

Ananias carried the precious icon to Athens. Although most Athenians in the first century A.D. were still pagans, they readily venerated the beautiful painting, calling it either the "Athenaia" or the "Athea."

The portrait remained in Athens until some time during the reign of Theodosius the Great (A.D. 375–395). A Christian named Basilius Soterichus received a vision of the Virgin, who instructed him to move her portrait to a new home, remote from the troubled cities of the Eastern Roman Empire. Soterichus, with a band of pilgrims, traveled hundreds of miles over land and sea seeking an appropriate location. At length they arrived at Mount Sumela in what is now northeastern Turkey near the fabled city of Trebizond (Trabzon). There they founded the Panagia Monastery. Panagia literally means "All Holy," but in the Eastern Orthodox Church it has in fact become synonymous with the Virgin Mary.

The existence of a monastery on Mount Sumela is confirmed by Greek Church history. Historical documents also confirm that it was founded in the late fourth century and was dedicated exclusively to Mary. There is growing evidence that the icon itself may have survived for hundreds of years and that it exists even today. An artifact that I am now researching is located in a remote corner of the Greek peninsula and corresponds remarkably to this legend.

What we do know, on the authority of the sixth-century chronicler Theodor Lector, is that a beautiful portrait of Mary was found in the mid-fifth century in Jerusalem. The discoverer of the portrait, according to Theodor, was the Empress of the Eastern Roman Empire, Athenaïs Eudokia, wife of Theodosius II. A common belief at the time and for centuries thereafter was that the portrait had been painted by the Apostle Luke, who was also held to be, in the legend related above, the painter of the portrait that supposedly was carried to the Panagia Monastery in northeastern Turkey. Could that portrait have turned up seventy-five years later in Jerusalem? It is not impossible.

Eudokia was noted for her blond beauty and for her intelligence. She wrote allegorical poetry, some of which survives to this day, and was instrumental in founding Constantinople's first college. Her father was an Athenian rhetorician named Leontius. Once converted, she was an ardent Christian, gaining fame as the era's most noted collector of early Christian relics.

According to historical records, the empress made at least two journeys to Jerusalem. The first, in A.D. 438–439, was a pilgrimage made in gratitude for the successful marriage of her daughter Eudocia to the Western Roman Emperor two years earlier. It seems unlikely that the empress discovered the portrait during that first visit, for there is no mention of it in the chronicles of the period when Eudokia shared the role of empress with Theodosius' sister Pulcheria. Eudokia fell from imperial favor around the year 440. She left Constantinople for Jerusalem and lived there until her death in 460. One account specifically notes that Eudokia sent the famous portrait to Saint Pulcheria, her sister-in-law, who died in 453.

We may never know if it was Empress Eudokia who found the *Theotókos Hodegetria,* as the icon was named. There is more general agreement that she did indeed find relics of Saint Peter and Saint Stephen during her first visit to Jerusalem in 438, and that she returned triumphantly with them to Constantinople. Perhaps because of the empress's fame as a relic hunter, the discovery of the early portrait of the Virgin was linked with her name.

Saint Pulcheria, while she was co-empress, is credited with the building of at least three churches in Constantinople dedicated to the Virgin Mary, one of which was named the Hodegetria. The name *Hodegetria* means "Pointer of the Way." Some believe that the portrait was located there where it "pointed the way" to a miraculous well. Others, who have looked at Byzantine paintings such as Our Lady of Saint Vladimir, in Moscow, that are believed to resemble the Hodegetria in general outline, point out that in all cases the Virgin points with her finger toward the Child she holds in her arms. In the Guadalupan Image, as noted earlier, the Christ Child is absent.

Bishop Photius, ninth-century Patriarch of Constantinople, has given us a description of the icon found in Jerusalem four centuries earlier:

A Virgin Mother carrying in her pure arms, for the common salvation of our kind, the Common Creator reclining as an infant . . . turning her eyes on her begotten Child in the affection of her heart.

The Hodegetria remained for centuries in the magnificent Church of Saint Sophia, built by Justinian and dedicated on Christmas Day, 538. According to a letter of Pope Innocent III written on January 13, 1207, as a result of the turmoil caused by the Fourth Crusade the famous portrait was moved to another church, Christ Pantocrator, which was favored by Roman Christians. The move was made just in time, for, as historian Edward Gibbon comments:

> trampled under foot [were] the most venerable objects of Christian worship. In the Cathedral of S. Sophia, the Ample Veil of the sanctuary was ripped asunder for the sake of its gold fringe; and the altar, a monument of art and riches, was broken into pieces and shared among the captors . . . a prostitute was seated on the throne of the Patriarch and . . . sung and danced in the Church to ridicule the hymns and processions of the Orientals.

A generally accepted view is that the Hodegetria was destroyed when the Turks conquered Constantinople in 1453. A contemporary record tells of a Turkish commander who had one of his soldiers flogged because he "ripped into four pieces and dragged through the mud" a painting sacred to the Christians.

Yet there is widespread belief in two alternative histories of the famous painting. Robert de Clari, a French

historian who accompanied the Fourth Crusade in the
sacking of Constantinople in 1204, reported that:

> Murzuphius . . . took with him the icon, an image of Our
> Lady which the Greeks call by this name [Hodegetria]
> and which the emperors carry with them when they go
> into battle . . . having as great a faith in this icon that
> they fully believe that no one who carries it can be
> defeated.

According to an old Venetian tradition, the famous painting was brought with other booty to Italy and installed in
Saint Mark's Basilica in Venice. De Clari lends some support to this view:

> When the Doge of Venice and the Venetians saw that
> they wanted to make my lord Henry of Flanders em-
> peror, they were against it, nor would they suffer it, un-
> less they should have a certain image of Our Lady which
> was painted on a panel. This image was rich beyond
> measure, and was all covered with rich and precious
> stones. And *the Greeks said that it was the first image of
> Our Lady ever made or painted.* The Greeks had such
> faith in this image that they treasured it above every-
> thing, and they bore it in procession every Sunday and
> they worshipped it and gave gifts to it. Now the Vene-
> tians were not willing to allow my lord Henry to be em-
> peror, unless they should have this image, so . . . it was
> given to them and . . . Henry was crowned. (italics
> added)

Doge Enrico Dandole, to whom the treasure was reput-
edly given, died before he could return to Venice, but

perhaps a colleague brought it back. In another letter of
Pope Innocent III (sometime after 1207), there is some
support for this view. The Pope never traveled to Constantinople, yet in his letter he praises the Hodegetria for
its miraculous beauty, writing that the painting contains
something of Mary's own soul. Such a description would
seem to indicate that the Pope had actually seen the famous icon.

Another strong tradition holds that the Hodegetria still
exists. Chroniclers claim that, early in the eighth century,
when the iconoclasts were bent on destroying all sacred
images, the Hodegetria was taken to a chapel deep in a
forest far outside Constantinople for safekeeping. According to official records, it was returned to Saint Sophia in
840, but how can we be certain that the original painting
was returned?

One story says that in truth the inhabitants of that distant forest kept the icon. A variant of this same story
holds that the Hodegetria was returned to Saint Sophia,
only to leave Constantinople once more, this time never
to return, when Princess Anna, sister of Emperor Basil II,
was married in 988 to Vladimir, Grand Duke of Russia
and a recent convert to the Eastern Orthodox Church.

Tradition says that the icon, which survives to this day
at Jasna Gora (Hill of Light) near Kraków, Poland, and
is known as Our Lady of Częstochowa, is in reality the
ancient Hodegetria. Just as Mexico's national symbol is
Our Lady of Guadalupe, so Poland's is Our Lady of
Częstochowa. It is linked to the Hodegetria through a
Ukrainian named Prince Ladislaus Opolszyk, who is

known to have existed historically and to have had ties with both Hungarian and Neapolitan nobility. The story goes that this prince brought the icon from the deep forest in what would be modern Hungary to Częstochowa, where a monastery grew up around it. The fleur-de-lis on the robe of Our Lady of Częstochowa is a typical motif of Neapolitan art. As mentioned earlier, fleur-de-lis also decorate the rose-colored robe of the Virgin of Guadalupe.

But an even more remarkable similarity between Our Lady of Częstochowa and the Image of Guadalupe lies in the darkness of the Virgin's complexion. The tradition of a "Black Madonna" has roots in the discovery by an Italian monk in the middle of the fourth century of three statues of Mary. He distributed these statues to churches in Italy and Sardinia. One, at the Santuario d'Oropa, northeast of Turin, exists to this day. About three feet high, it is made of cedarwood. The dark-faced Virgin carries the Christ Child and her arms are lifted in prayer.

Worship of the *Vierge Noire* was especially widespread in medieval France. Shrines to the Black Madonna can still be found at Avioth, Le Puy, Moulins, and Marsat. There are several in Spain also, including a famous one at the Benedictine Abbey of Montserrat.

The dark color of the skin of Our Lady of Częstochowa did not arise from the oxidation of silver in the pigment of the paint but from smoke from charcoal burning. The olive complexion of the Virgin of Guadalupe, on the other hand, seems to have been there from the first and is not the result of aging or smoke.

What of the Hodegetria, the famous early painting of

the Virgin? A seventeenth-century scholar from Chartres, Vincent Sablon, found a description of the portrait in the works of a fourteenth-century Byzantine historian named Necephorus Callistos:

> Necephorus, however, says he saw several paintings made from nature by Saint Luke, in which the color of her [Mary's] skin was the color of wheat—which is probably to say that when wheat is ripe it tends to be brownish, or a chestnut color.

Mexicans have for centuries considered this brownish or chestnut color to be the identifying characteristic of the Virgin of Guadalupe. In fact, they have named the image "La Morena," meaning "the dark-complexioned woman."

In this regard they echo an ancient Greek tradition. As noted by Anna Brownell Jameson, a nineteenth-century writer:

> To this day, the Neapolitan lemonade-seller will allow no other than a formal Greek Madonna, with olive-green complexion and veiled head, to be set up in his booth.

"It is," Jameson continues, "the *dark-colored, ancient Greek Madonnas such as this which all along have been credited miraculous* . . . Guido, who himself painted lovely Madonnas, went every Saturday to pray before the little black Madonna de la Guardia and we are assured held this old Eastern relic in devout veneration" (italics added).

Perhaps the fact that the Virgin of Guadalupe was one in a long chain of "dark Virgins" was the reason why Archbishop Montufar defended its authenticity in that first inquiry in 1556. The color, whether "black," "chestnut," or "Indian olive," was no accident. For it is by means of this unique characteristic that the ancient Madonnas were "credited miraculous."

Was it because the icon she discovered in Jerusalem was dark of hue that Empress Eudokia, her sister-in-law Saint Pulcheria, and then all Byzantium came to pay it homage? Let us suppose that the color of the Virgin's complexion in the Hodegetria was indeed what produced the ardor in the Byzantines, the connection between them dimmed into forgetfulness with the passage of a thousand years. Let us also grant that the same skin color appears in both the Hodegetria and the Virgin of Guadalupe. What might this have to do with either being an authentic representation of the Virgin Mary? The answer comes by recalling that Mary was a Jew.

Just as I was completing the research for this study, I found myself paging through a compilation of old Hebrew themes, newly translated from ancient sources. My eyes focused on a tiny footnote translating, from the Aramaic *Babylonian Talmud* (c. A.D. 475), a statement about the supreme beauty of Queen Esther, of Old Testament fame. I was astonished:

Her skin was greenish, like the skin of a myrtle.

Precisely the same can be said about the skin tone of the Virgin of Guadalupe.

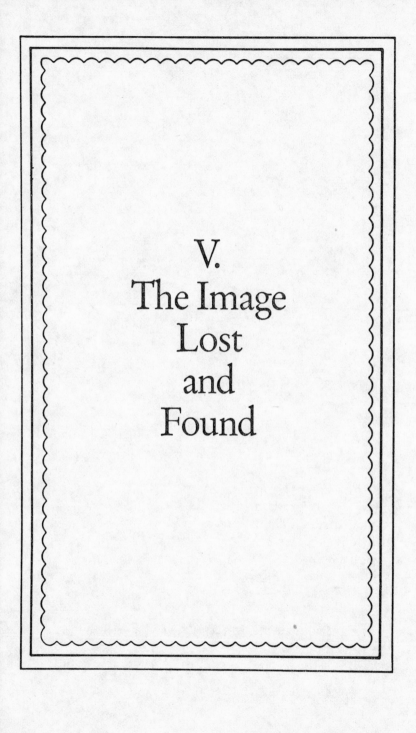

V.
The Image
Lost
and
Found

> Now a great sign appeared in heaven: a woman,
> adorned with the sun, standing on the moon, and
> with the twelve stars on her head for a crown.

Revelation 12:1

THE IMAGE OF GUADALUPE IS LINKED, IN A SURPRISING
way, to the early icons brought to Constantinople by the
Empress Eudokia and others in the fifth century. Two
hundred years later a young monk, who had spent several
years in Constantinople, brought to Rome a statue of the
Virgin that apparently resembled the one now in the Santuario d'Oropa, near Turin. The young monk, who later
became Pope Gregory the Great, carried the statue
around Rome, using it as a palladium—a religious object
to counteract evil. The statue was credited with ending a
plague then rampant in Rome. Later, Pope Gregory gave
the statue to Saint Leander of Spain.

The story picks up again more than six hundred years
later, in the fourteenth century. According to papers
about the victory of the Christians over the Moors at
Salido in 1340, Spanish King Alfonso XI credited his success to a discovery made in 1328. In that year the Virgin
appeared before a shepherd named Gil Cordero and
directed him to search a cave, by a river, on the plain of

Estremadura. There he discovered a well-preserved statue of the Virgin.

The name of that river translates as "hidden channel." We know it better as Guadalupe.

A Hieronymite monastery was established there under the tutelage of Cardinal Don Pedro Barroso. Before long, the surrounding community grew into the town of Guadalupe. In it could be found the richest museum in all Europe. The museum was visited and generously supported by royalty and such notables of the fifteenth and sixteenth centuries as Columbus, Cortés, and Admiral Andrea Doria. The opulent monastery and museum of Guadalupe reigned supreme for more than a century, being gradually eclipsed only by the Escorial of Philip II in the late sixteenth century.

According to manuscripts in the Monastery Archives and the Spanish National Library, the statue of Our Lady of Guadalupe-Estremadura was twice hidden. It was first put away for safekeeping in Byzantine times. It was hidden again in A.D. 711, at the beginning of the Muslim invasion of Spain. Historian Jacques LaFaye quotes from an anonymous Codex dated A.D. 1440. It tells of:

> . . . that time when all the Christians fled from Seville. Among them were some saintly priests who took with them a statue of Our Lady, Holy Mary . . . and in these mountains the priests dug a cave that they surrounded with large gravestones; inside they placed the statue of Our Lady, Holy Mary, together with a small bell and a reliquary containing a writing which told how this statue of Holy Mary had been offered at Rome to the Arch-

bishop of Seville, Saint Leander, by the Doctor of the Church, Saint Gregory.

LaFaye notes that another part of the Codex describes how an apparition of Mary led the shepherd to discover the statue. Although LaFaye believes that the statue is genuinely ancient, he doubts its association with Saints Gregory and Leander, and completely dismisses the idea of any apparition. Instead, he points out the many similarities in the legends concerning discovery of the Estremaduran statue and the Mexican Image. He believes that the story of the Virgin's apparition before Juan Diego and the miraculous appearance of her image on his tilma is an echo of the story surrounding the discovery of the Virgin's statue in Spain two hundred years earlier.

Yet the similarities in the two legends can just as easily be used to support the actuality of apparitions at the two sites, and incidentally to confirm the early existence of a shrine on Tepeyac hill. This is indicated indirectly by the testimony given at the official inquiry in 1556, when Alonso de Santiago, one of those objecting to Archbishop Montufar's approval of the Virgin of Guadalupe, said:

> The Archbishop ought to have sent orders to that hermitage, that it not bear the name "Our Lady of Guadalupe" but "of Tepeaca or Tepeaquilla"; because, if in Spain Our Lady of Guadalupe was so named, it was because there was there a town so named.

Not only does Santiago's testimony provide independent confirmation of the existence of a shrine on Tepeyac hill, but it gives a clue as to why the name given to the shrine should be so controversial. For ostensibly there was no reason why the Mexican shrine should not have been named the Virgin of Tepeyac. The fact that it was instead named the Virgin of Guadalupe indicates that something surely out of the ordinary happened on that Mexican hilltop.

The story of the discovery of the Spanish statue was well known at the time. Is there any reason to doubt that Guadalupe was chosen as the name for the Mexican shrine on Tepeyac because, as in Spain, an apparition of the Virgin occurred there?

Whatever the skepticism expressed by historians over the centuries, the people continued to believe in the miraculous nature of the Image of Guadalupe. One evidence of that belief, and the growing acceptance of the Image by Church authorities, is the widespread dispersal of copies of the Image throughout the western hemisphere and even in Europe.

I have already mentioned the copy of the Virgin of Guadalupe that was carried on Admiral Giovanni Andrea Doria's ship in the famous sea battle of Lepanto. That copy, believed to be the earliest copy still extant, now hangs on the wall high above the altar of Santo Stefano d'Aveto in Italy, where I viewed it in the spring of 1981.

It is not quite three feet in height—about half the size of the original, which measures 66 by 41 inches. I climbed a twenty-five-foot ladder to get within four feet of the picture. Close study reveals that every detail of the copy is identical with the original, including the number of stars on the mantle—forty-six—the number of years it took to build the temple in Jerusalem. The only exception is the shape and color of the gold rays and crown. These appear more skillfully done in the copy than in the original. In any case, it is now recognized that the gold rays were added to the original at a later date, and may have been retouched at various times in the past.

In 1580, only a few years after this famous copy of the Image was carried to Europe, a portrait of the Virgin was painted by an anonymous artist on the wall of an adobe hut belonging to an Indian. Although the hut was inundated by the terrible floods that submerged much of Mexico City for five years, the picture on the wall survived. A shrine to hold the wall painting was built in 1595 and named Our Lady of the Angels. The painting and the shrine still exist.

Our Lady of the Angels resembles the Image of Guadalupe in several striking details. The mantle is identical —blue with a gold border and sprinkled with gold stars. The only difference is that in Our Lady of the Angels the mantle does not cover the Virgin's head. The robe, too, is the same—rose-colored with gold fleur-de-lis. And the clasp at the throat is identical—oval-shaped with a cross in the middle. In both paintings gold rays surround the figure and under the Virgin's feet is a crescent moon.

Many of these motifs are derived from a description of the Virgin given in the Bible in Revelation 12. Besides the golden rays of the sun surrounding her and the moon at her feet, the Bible passage mentions a golden crown, present in both pictures. Such Revelation 12 motifs appear in portraits of the Virgin dating back at least to the eighth century. But it is important to remember that these particular details—the gold rays, stars and border of the mantle, the gold crown, the gold fleur-de-lis on the robe, and the moon and angel at her feet—are now known to be later additions. Comparison of the Image with Our Lady of the Angels would seem to indicate that those additions were made in the late sixteenth century.

Since then, literally millions of copies of the Virgin of Guadalupe have found their way into the hands of worshippers. One of the earliest pieces of printed matter in the New World is a small line engraving of the Image that must have been distributed by the thousands to the newly converted Christians of Central America. In the eighteenth century famous painters like Miguel Cabrera produced a series of paintings illustrating the legend of Juan Diego, and these too were copied widely. In the nineteenth century the Emperor Maximilian, a devoted believer in the Virgin of Guadalupe, had her image stamped on banners that hung in his court and engraved on medals he presented to his soldiers.

The historian Northrop was struck by the overwhelming influence of the Image on Christian worship in Mexico. He wrote:

Anyone who has walked among the mountains or through the fields and orchards of Switzerland, Bavaria, Austria, or France will recall coming again and again, even in out-of-the-way places, upon little shrines of the Christ hanging upon the Cross. This is the true and natural symbol for orthodox Catholicism. Nevertheless, in

journeys covering hundreds of miles radiating from Mexico City in every direction, no such image of the Christ
located in the countryside or even made very conspicuous in the churches comes to mind; in its place appears
instead the Madonna of Guadalupe.

Despite religious and, later, political opposition to the
Virgin of Guadalupe, the ardent devotion the painting inspired has never flagged. In the earliest history of New
Spain, written by a Franciscan who was beloved by the
Indians and became known by the name "Motolinia"
(threadbare), there is a remarkable account of the unprecedented conversion of the Aztecs to Christianity,
which seems to have occurred a few years after 1531, the
date historians now pinpoint as the year when the miraculous Image of the Virgin appeared on Juan Diego's
tilma.
Motolinia claimed five million conversions, and described the method he used to arrive at this estimate:

[I] calculate the number of the baptized in two ways:
first, by the towns and provinces which have been baptized; and second, by the number of priests who have ad-
ministered the Sacrament . . . From the sixty who are
here in this year 1536, I subtract twenty who have not
baptized because they are new to the country and do not
know the language. For the forty who remain, I would
estimate one hundred thousand baptisms each . . . there
must have been baptized up to the present day, nearly
five million.

By 1541, Motolinia says that some nine million Aztecs had become Christians. Although he makes no direct reference to an apparition of the Virgin at the site or to a shrine there containing the Image, he does make specific reference to Tepeyacac, an alternate spelling for Tepeyac:

> Since this report was copied, over five hundred thousand have been baptized . . . in 1537 in the province of Tepeyacac alone, there have been baptized by actual count over sixty thousand souls.

A popular theory among those who doubt the supernatural origin of the Image of Guadalupe is that the Church commissioned the picture and invented the legend of Juan Diego to account for it, as a device to attract the Indians to Christianity. Yet the fierce jealousies between the Spanish religious authorities that are described in Motolinia's *History of the Indians of New Spain* would seem to argue against a Church conspiracy to invent a useful "miracle." For such a conspiracy to be effective, a certain measure of unanimity on the part of the Church fathers would have been essential. The dissension revealed by the official inquiry of 1556, with its open hostility to the growing devotion to Guadalupe, is a further reason to doubt that the Church "concocted" the miracle on Tepeyac hill.

Motolinia's writings contain tantalizingly indirect references to that miracle. He speaks of "strange things" that happened "ten or twelve years" before the publication of his history in 1541. In a later comment, he reports that he has heard of these strange occurrences, but he "neither confirms nor denies" their actuality.

The ambiguity of Church authorities toward the Virgin of Guadalupe has gradually given way to wholehearted acceptance. By the time of the second official inquiry in 1666 attempts were already being made to give solid scientific support to the miraculous nature of the painting which had inspired such widespread devotion among the common people of Mexico. By the nineteenth century some of the highest figures in the Church and the government, including Emperor Maximilian, were enthusiastic Guadalupans.

The foundation for historical research on the Image was laid in the eighteenth century by Siguenza y Gongora, a professor of mathematics who had been given an entire portfolio of ancient Indian documents by his royal friend, Don Juan de Alva Ixtlilcóatl. Alva Ixtlilcóatl, who had received these treasures from his father, lacked an heir, so he bequeathed the portfolio to Siguenza, to be given in turn to the Mexican National Library.

Although there is disagreement as to how much mention was made of the painting in this portfolio, there undoubtedly was some reference to it, for the Ixtlilcóatls, father and son, believed implicitly in the miracle on Tepeyac hill. When Siguenza, who had been skeptical, read through the documents, he also was convinced.

In 1746, the historian Beneducci Boturini published a history of New Spain based on a wealth of sixteenth-century documents which he had gathered together. Of all

those who have tried to trace the history of the Image,
Boturini was one of the most enthusiastic:

> Hardly had I arrived in Mexico when I felt myself driven
> by an invariable attraction to undertake research into the
> prodigious miracles of Our Lady of Guadalupe. I discov-
> ered that its history was based on *a single tradition,* and
> that it was not known where or into whose hands the
> written proof of such a great prodigy had fallen. (italics
> added)

Even scholars who dismiss the idea of a supernatural
origin for the painting are grateful for Boturini's surviving documents. Among them is a list of thirty-one sources
confirming the apparition of Mary in 1531. Boturini spent
seven years compiling the list which he published in his
Prólogo Galeato. His famous *Museum Catalogue of Indian History* also contains significant Guadalupan references. He was later expelled from Mexico for political
reasons, and it is tragic that he was already dead when
the King of Spain appointed him "Historiographer of the
Indies."

Despair almost surely was a major factor in his death.
His thirty-one Guadalupan sources were confiscated by
the Mexican authorities, along with the rest of his scholarship, at the time of his expulsion. The documents survived, but their elaboration, known only to Boturini, did
not.

Eventually, the Boturini Collection came into the
hands of a Mexican aristocrat, M. F. de Echeverría y Vei-

1. The Image of Guadalupe, imprinted on Juan Diego's tilma (cloak) made from agave (maguey) cactus. Since 1531, the year of the apparitions of the Lady to Juan Diego, this Image has been the source of faith, strength, and awe for millions of people. *(Photo courtesy Luis Carlos Pérez Cavilan)*

The Image of Guadalupe is just one in a long line of portraits of the Mother of Jesus which have survived the ages.

2. Another is Our Lady of Częstochowa, preserved in the Shrine of Jasna Gora in Poland. Legend says that this is an actual portrait of the Virgin Mary done by Saint Luke on a cypress tabletop from the House in Nazareth. Science says that this beautiful painting can factually be dated as far back as the fifth or sixth century. *(Photo courtesy the National Shrine of Our Lady of Częstochowa, Doylestown, Pennsylvania)*

3. This beautiful icon is a characteristic *hodegetria* — "pointer of the way" (the Madonna's fingers point to the Infant Christ). It can be found in a church in Thessalonika which bears the intriguing title Sanctuary of the Acheiropoietos ("not made with human hands"). *(Author's photo)*

4, 5. The Tribute Roll, section 1, on amate paper, executed about 1530, showing (closeup) the Virgin of Guadalupe located at the year 1531 by the Aztec Disc. This is the Codex Saville, a pre-Columbian Mexican pictorial calendar, painted on paper made of treated fibers from the agave (maguey) cactus, the same plant that supplied the cloth for Juan Diego's tilma. See the Codex Saville in the Appendices. *(Photo courtesy the Museum of the American Indian, Heye Foundation)*

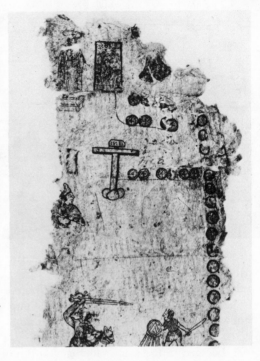

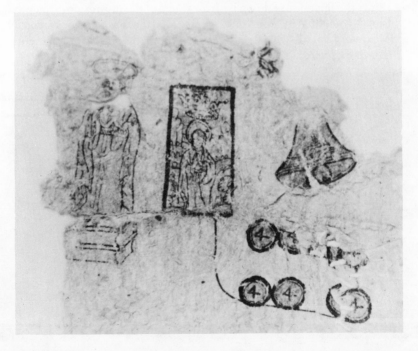

6. This large mural is located in the small sanctuary atop Tepeyac Hill, the site of the apparitions. It shows Juan Diego's first encounter with the Lady. In addition to the angels, note especially the agave cactus placed significantly between the two figures, and the songbirds, none of which is indigenous to Mexico. (*Author's photo*)

7. Located in the same sanctuary as the preceding, this large mural shows the famous unfolding by Juan Diego of the mysteriously painted tilma. Kneeling in front of the Image is the Franciscan Bishop of Mexico, Juan de Zumarraga. Note the authentic Aztec haircuts. (*Author's photo*)

8. Views of Our Lady of Guadalupe. Left, a full-size reproduction of the mantle of Our Lady of Guadalupe from negatives taken by a photographer at the basilica. Right, a painting depicting Juan Diego unfolding his mantle to show Bishop Zumarraga the roses from Tepeyac Hill. (*Photos courtesy National Catholic News Service*)

9. There are literally hundreds of representations of the Image of Guadalupe in Mexico City alone, this one near the Church of San Diego, adjacent to a museum commemorating the Mexican-American War and the Treaty of Guadalupe-Hidalgo. The Latin words mean "To no other nation has been accorded such honor," and were said by Pope Benedict XIV in 1754 as he proclaimed the Virgin of Guadalupe patron of Mexico. The two cultures of Mexico are never far apart, as can be noted by the Aztec goddess atop the gate. *(Author's photo)*

10. A group of pilgrims crowds a Mexico City street near the basilica. About five thousand pilgrims pray before the Image every weekday and almost a hundred thousand on Sundays. The basilica draws more than a million people on the feast of Our Lady of Guadalupe, December 12. *(Photo courtesy of National Catholic News Service)*

11. The Church of the Well (east of Tepeyac Hill), so named for the still-usable water source it surrounds. This church was built about two hundred years ago, but the site has long been associated with both the first Guadalupan Hermitage and the grave of Juan Diego. (*Author's photo*)

12. The old Basilica of Our Lady of Guadalupe, Mexico City. After more than four hundred years the building had settled so much that it was declared unsafe and a new basilica was planned. (*Photo courtesy Religious News Service*)

13. The new Basilica of Our Lady of Guadalupe, dedicated on October 12, 1976. *(Photo courtesy Milton M. Knight)*

14. The high altar of the new basilica. The Image of Guadalupe is encased in a glass frame on the wall behind the altar. *(Photo courtesy Milton M. Knight)*

15. The author Jody Brant Smith (right) and Dr. Robert L. Bucklin, a forensic pathologist for Los Angeles County and a member of the Image of Guadalupe Research Project, Inc., during a break in the photographing of the Image. *(Photo courtesy Milton M. Knight)*

16. Setting up the camera in front of the Image to take the infrared photographs for spectroscopic examination. *(Author's photo)*

17. Dr. José Aste-Tonsmann, author of a recent book on the eyes of the Image of Guadalupe, at a symposium examining his work with computer enhancements of the Image. *(Author's photo)*

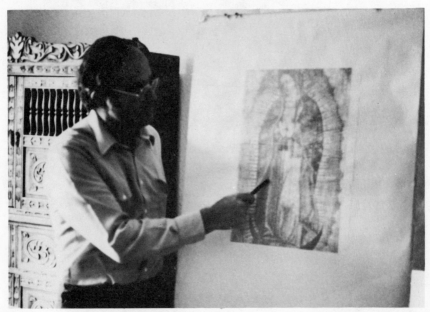

18. Closeup of the face of the Image of Guadalupe. It is the eyes that have fascinated scientists for over a half century, ever since the "human bust" was first discovered. (*Author's photo*)

These photographs show computer-enhanced printouts and enlargements of the eyes of the Image. The computer only enlarges what is already there. It does not add anything that is not already present in the subject.

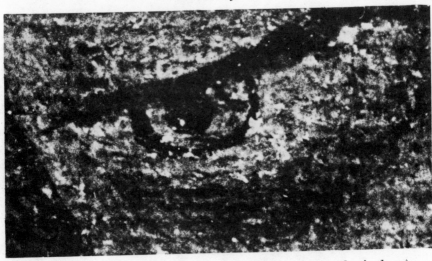

19. The right eye of the Image, magnified ten times. *(Author's photo)*

20. The location of the figures in the right eye, outlined in white for clarity. Note particularly the large figure at the right, the "human bust" that was discovered over fifty years ago. *(Photo courtesy Dr. José Aste-Tonsmann)*

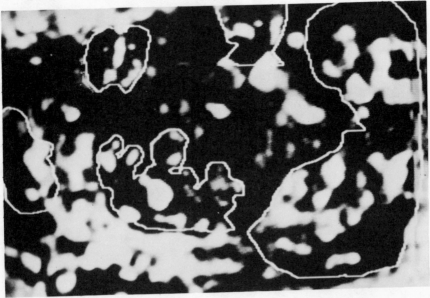

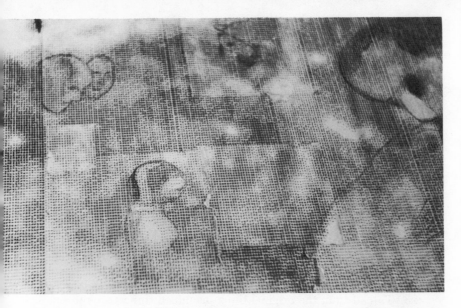

21. Computer-enhanced printout of the right eye. Again, in the upper right-hand corner, see the "human bust." Compare this to photo 20. (*Author's photo*)

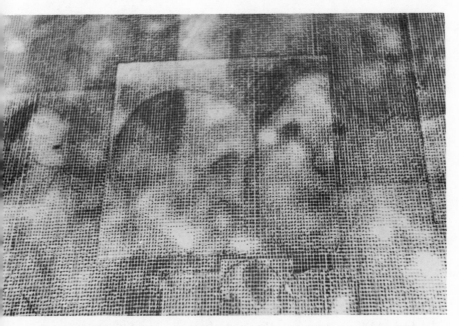

22. Computer-enhanced printout of the left eye. Again, on the left, the outline of the Indian woman. (*Author's photo*)

23. Thread from the original tilma magnified three hundred times. *(Author's photo)*

24. From the Codex Telleriano-Remensis. Note the remarkable specification of the year 1531. The Spanish reads: "In this year of the reed 1531 came an eclipse of the sun." Note also Halley's Comet depicted in background. *(From Anthony F. Aveni,* Skywatchers of Ancient Mexico)

25. Our Lady of Guadalupe of Estremadura. This Spanish Black Madonna plays a pivotal role in the evolution of the Guadalupan mystery. *(Turn-of-the-century depiction of ancient statue.)*

26. The first visit outside the Vatican by the new pope, John Paul II, was to Puebla, Mexico, to a meeting of Central and South American bishops, and then to the Basilica of Our Lady of Guadalupe in January 1979. In late 1981, this larger-than-life statue was installed in the old basilica courtyard in memory of his stay. (*Author's photo*)

tia. Echeverría was not originally a believer in the miraculous Image. What caused him to reassess his views? It must have been some document he found in the Boturini Collection, for immediately after receiving it he became a vigorous proponent. The Boturini Collection now rests in the archives of the Basilica of Our Lady of Guadalupe in Mexico City.

At the beginning of Mexico's war of independence from Spain in 1810, the revolutionary leader, Father Hidalgo, a parish priest who had been greatly influenced by the French Revolution, adopted the Image of Guadalupe as the revolutionary symbol. The treaty which ended the Mexican-American War of 1846–48 was named the Treaty of Guadalupe-Hidalgo, further evidence of the overwhelming devotion accorded the Image in the nineteenth century.

In the twentieth century scholars have brought to light several additional documents which, while they do not prove that an apparition of the Virgin actually occurred in 1531, do support the view that belief in the apparition was widely held at the time. Church leaders today no longer quarrel with that belief, which has persisted with undiminished strength through the centuries. On October 12, 1945, Pope Pius XII specifically confirmed the Church's view by stating:

On the shores of Lake Texcoco flowered the Miracle, and on the cloak . . . was painted a most lovely Portrait, by brushes not of this earth . . .

In 1976 a new basilica was built in Mexico City to house the sacred painting. There, in January of 1979, the newly designated Pope, John Paul II, made clear that the Roman Catholic Church now accepted, without reservation, the importance of the Virgin of Guadalupe in the spiritual life of Mexico.

VI.
The
Right
Eye
of the
Virgin

> The highest that man can attain in these matters is
> wonder.
>
> Goethe

IN ADDITION TO MY SEARCH FOR HISTORICAL EVIDENCE
that would confirm or deny the truth of the Guadalupan
legend, I wanted to find out what kinds of scientific
research had already been done on the painting. One of
the most tantalizing leads I followed concerned what
seems to be the reflected image of a man's head in the
right eye of the Virgin.

Anyone who examines the painting close up can see
this apparent reflection. How long it has been part of the
painting no one knows, for documented note of it did not
occur until 1929 (Marcué), and it was not until after
1951, when the anomaly was rediscovered by Carlos
Salinas, that scientific examination was made.

One of those called in to examine this particular aspect
of the sacred Image was an ophthalmologist, Dr. Javier
Torroella-Bueno. What he discovered is truly amazing.

Before I could understand the importance of his discovery I needed to learn something about the physiology
of the human eye, in particular what is called the Purkinje-Sanson principle (named after Jan Evangelista Pur-

kinje, Czech physiologist, and Louis Joseph Sanson,
French physician, who independently described the phenomenon). In its simplest form, the Purkinje-Sanson law
states that whenever we see any object, the object is
reflected in each eye, not once but in three different
places. This threefold reflection is caused by the curvature of the eye's cornea. Two of the reflections are always
right side up and one is always upside down. Depending
on the angle at which the object is seen, the three reflections occur on different parts of the eye, because of the
differing angles of curvature of the cornea. The curvature
also causes the reflected images to be distorted in a vary-
ing degree.

On May 26, 1956, Dr. Torroella sent the following letter to Carlos Salinas:

> If we take a light source and put it in front of the eye
> . . . we see the cornea, the only part of the eye which
> can reflect an image in three places [images of Purkinje-
> Sanson]: the front surface of the cornea, and both front
> and rear of the lens surfaces, immediately behind . . .
> The image of the Virgin of Guadalupe, which has been
> given to me for study, contains in the cornea these reflec-
> tions . . . In the images in question, there is a perfect
> collocation in agreement with this [principle], the distor-
> tion of the figures even concurring with the predicted
> curvature of the cornea.

In other words, in the eyes of the Virgin of Guadalupe,
not only is the cornea curved but it is curved exactly the
way the human eye is curved. The location of the reflections, which can be seen in both eyes, conforms exactly to

what occurs in the living eye. One is near the temple while in the other eye the reflection is near the bridge of the nose. Thus the images are said to be "collocated"— that is, they are located where they would have to be in order to conform to the way our eyes work together to perceive a single object.

Dr. Torroella's findings were corroborated by another ophthalmologist, Dr. Rafael Torija-Lavoignet, who invited me to his office to discuss the conclusions he had reached on examining the painting twenty-five years earlier. He gave me a copy of a statement published in 1956:

> When the ophthalmoscopic light is directed to the pupil of the human eye, one sees a luminous reflection . . . Lighting the pupil of the eye of the Image of the Virgin, there appears the same luminous reflection . . . impossible to obtain on a simple surface, and moreover on one opaque, as [is] the said painting . . . I, with the aid of the ophthalmoscope, proceeded to examine the eyes of diverse paintings, even of photographs (in each case, they were of readily distinguishable persons), but I found no reflections in any of them.

Two years later, September 20, 1958, Dr. Torija published his study of the Purkinje-Sanson effect as exhibited in the Guadalupan painting. The "human bust" reflection is readily visible, he states, especially in the cornea of the right eye. "In addition to the human bust," continues Torija, "there are two luminous reflections, which together correspond to the three images of Purkinje-Sanson."

Dr. Torija explained to me that it is necessary to dilate the eye in order to perceive the second of the three reflections. After making precise measurement of the three face reflections he saw in the right eye of the Virgin, Dr. Torija concluded that they conformed perfectly with the requirements of the Purkinje-Sanson Law.

In his published study he states that "the human bust . . . image reflected in the cornea is not an optical illusion caused by some irregularity in the weave of the ayate [cactus cloth]." Dr. Torija made clear to me that he was not denying that there might be an imperfection in the weave, but that the way the eye of the painting reflected the light of the ophthalmoscope was exactly the way the curvature of the human eye reflected the same light. In other words, whether the reflections in the eye of the Virgin are caused by an irregularity in the coarse cactus cloth is essentially irrelevant.

Dr. Torija is convinced that the Image of Guadalupe is a miraculous creation. Additional research in the intervening years has buttressed this conviction.

In 1975 the glass was removed so the picture could be examined by another ophthalmologist, Dr. Enrique Graue. Dr. Graue reported: "The total sensation is that of seeing a 'living eye' and, really, it cannot be thought less than something supernatural."

An even more astonishing discovery was made two years ago by Dr. José Aste-Tonsmann, who received his doctorate in systems engineering from Cornell University. Using a photograph of the Image marked off in one-millimeter squares and using computer amplification to maging Bishop Zumárraga and the translator Juan González, and were imprinted in the left eye of the picture at the

I am not sure. Do the "human figures" perhaps constitute no more than one would be led to expect statistically? Are they but chance phenomena? Or is there a still more fundamental objection, that there are no figures in the eyes, nothing to "explain" in the first place? By this view, the putative shapes are projections only. The phenomena would then constitute a sort of Rorschach test.

But if, on the other hand, the figures are indeed genuine, then we are presented with a double helping of mystery. The Image of Guadalupe itself is said to be *acheiropoietos* —not made with human hands—and if the shapes in the eye are real, then they provide additional valuable evidence of such natural phenomena, for they too are "not made with human hands."

We know too little about the nature of perception itself to provide a conclusive answer. I find myself troubled with the idea of "reflections" of supposedly near subjects requiring microscopic enlargement to be even seen. Yet the possibility of Purkinje-Sanson phenomena remains intriguing.

It should be noted that hesitation about the eye figures (the study of which is a legitimate part of any history of the Guadalupe mystery) is not antireligious. The projection view is in fact the opinion of Father Rahm, mentioned above. The Church has always avoided falling into the hands of its enemies precisely by choosing to conduct its own rigorous tests of possible miracles well in advance of endorsing them.

VII.
Science
and the
Miraculous

You yourself are even another little world, and have within you the sun and moon and also the stars.

Origen, *Liviticum Homiliae*

THE BASILICA AUTHORITIES HAD AGREED TO ALLOW US TO make a close examination of the painting with the glass removed and to take infrared photographs of it, provided we avoided exposing the picture to excessive heat. The hot lights usually required for photography were out of the question. We arranged to use special lights that threw off little heat and to monitor the surface of the painting continuously with a thermometer.

The date was set for our long-awaited rendezvous—May 4, 1979. Dr. Callahan and I arrived in Mexico City four days earlier to make sure the cameras, lights, and other equipment necessary for our examination of the Guadalupe had been assembled and were in perfect working order.

What would we find when we viewed the Image close at hand? What would infrared reveal? Would new scientific techniques solve the mysteries surrounding the painting?

Philip Callahan and I had little sleep the night before. In the early evening of Friday, May 4, after the basilica

had been closed to worshippers, we arrived at the administration building behind the new basilica as arranged,
only to meet with disappointment. The Image could not
be viewed that evening because only two people knew
the combination to the huge vault where the painting
was kept when it was not on display. One of the two,
Abbot D. Guillermo Schulenburg-Prado, was out of the
country on business. The other, the new church's archi-
tect, refused to open the vault without direct authoriza-
tion of the abbot. We would have to wait until the abbot
returned on Monday.

To fill time and satisfy our curiosity we decided to visit
the chapel on top of Mount Tepeyac. Scenes of Juan
Diego's life were depicted on the wall panels in the foyer
to the main sanctuary. On examining one panel, Dr.
Callahan exclaimed: "Now I'm sure they'll let us photograph the Guadalupe on Monday."

Puzzled, I asked him the reason for his certainty. He
pointed to three birds in the panel. "I owned birds of
the same species when I was a boy," he explained, "and
not a one is a native to the Americas. It has to be a good
omen."

He was right. On Monday morning the young woman
who had been assigned to be our translator informed us
that the glass cover would be removed from the painting
late that same evening. "But don't tell anyone," she cau-
tioned, "anyone at all what is going to happen tonight—
especially not the press. If the newspapers find out, someone might put 'Yanquis Invade National Symbol' in three-
inch letters on the front page."

Unfortunately, on the preceding Friday we had given a preliminary interview to a reporter from United Press International. We worried the entire day that news of this interview would reach the basilica authorities.

At eight o'clock on Monday, May 7, 1979, Dr. Callahan and I arrived at the entrance to the basilica's administration building, where we were to meet our translator. Except for an occasional late pilgrim or night watchman, we were alone.

The minutes crawled by. Dr. Callahan stopped pacing and sat down on the steps of the old basilica, where the Guadalupe had reposed until 1976, when the church was closed because it had become structurally unsafe. Equally distraught, I climbed the wide steps leading up to another sanctuary, high on a hill behind the administrative building. I looked out over the city, then returned to the plaza below, where Callahan sat with his head buried in his hands.

Abruptly, out of the darkness of an underground garage, our translator appeared, along with several men in clerical garb. I had met most of them. As Dr. Callahan and I were guided to the upper floor of the church, several of our escorts expressed their apprehension concerning what was soon to occur.

Callahan, a Catholic, asked to receive Communion, and his wish was granted. Then we watched while a huge stainless steel door was opened and twelve men slid the life-sized painting backward into the vault.

In the old basilica, which was built in the early eighteenth century, there was no vault behind the Image.

Anyone who wished to examine the picture at close range was required to stand on a specially constructed platform, a cumbersome arrangement at best.

It took the twelve-man crew two hours to remove the heavily bejeweled outer frame, then the bulletproof glass, and finally the inner frame. While some of the men carefully placed the silver-backed picture in the position we had requested, others washed the glass and still others bustled around looking for electric outlets for our lights. We loaded our three cameras and rehearsed procedure. Then we set to work.

We first examined the picture with the naked eye and with a hand lens, from less than a half inch from the surface. We saw immediately that the gold rays surrounding the figure were badly chipped and scarred. The clerics must have noted the disappointment on our faces, for they quickly reminded us that the metallic gold rays were a later addition to the painting and were in no way indicative of the substance of the original Image.

In the pages that follow I am going to quote extensively from Dr. Callahan, with his kind permission. Regarding the gold used in the painting, he reports:

The gold paint of the sun-rays is metallic gold, opaque to near infrared rays, and that of the stars, et cetera, of the mantle are of an unknown pigment (probably alumina hydrate natural earth ocher) . . . these details were added by human hands long after the original painting was formed . . . the sun-rays, stars, and mantle trim will . . . deteriorate with time.

Our close examination with the naked eye confirmed the remarkable state of preservation of the original. There is no evidence whatsoever of cracking. Yet paintings less than half the age of the Guadalupe commonly show a web of hairline cracks across their entire surface, caused by drying of the paint. Any moisture left in the paint, or whatever was used to color the Image, would surely have evaporated in the four hundred and fifty years of its existence.

Another remarkable aspect of the painting which is immediately apparent to the naked eye is the way it seems to change both size and coloration when viewed from various distances. Dr. Callahan, who has studied the phenomenon of iridescence on bird feathers and insect scales, explains that this strange effect is caused by the diffraction of light from the surface:

Beyond six or seven feet . . . the skin tone becomes what might best be termed an olive-green, an "Indian Olive," or gray-green tone. It would seem that somehow the gray and "caked"-looking white pigment of face and hands combines with the rough surface of unsized tilma to "collect" light, and diffract from afar the olive-skinned hue . . . Such a technique would seem to be impossible to accomplish by human hands; however, it occurs often in nature. In the coloring of bird feathers and butterfly scales, and on the *electra* of brightly colored beetles. Such colors are physically diffracted . . . do not depend on absorption and reflection from molecular pigments, but rather on the "surface-sculpturing" of the feather or the butterfly scales.

Callahan concludes:

> The same physical effect is quite evident in the face of
> the *Imagen*, and is easily observed by slowly backing
> away from the Painting until the details of the imper-
> fections of the tilma fabric are no longer visible. At a dis-
> tance where the pigment and the "surface-sculpturing"
> blend together, the overwhelming beauty of the olive-
> colored Madonna emerges . . . the expression suddenly
> appears reverent yet joyous, Indian, yet European, olive-
> skinned, yet white of hue . . . It is a face that inter-
> mingles the Christianity of Byzantine Europe with the
> overpowering naturalism of the New World Indian.

After our preliminary examination, we took seventy-
five photographs, forty of which were on specially prepared infrared film. We made both full-figure shots and
extreme closeups of the face, hands, and other areas of
special interest. Working past midnight into the early
morning, we spent four hours with the mysterious painting—probably a longer stretch of time for uninterrupted
examination than was available even to the artists and
physicians who took part in the official inquiry of 1666.

At dawn I was on a plane bound for my home in Pensacola, Dr. Callahan was in another plane, his destination
Gainesville, also in Florida, but several hundred miles
southeast. He carried with him the precious film, and he
had taken special precautions to ensure its safety during
preboarding and customs inspections. A few days later, I
was present in his darkroom when he developed the film.
Our excitement grew as we waited for the developer to
work.

The first picture developed appeared fuzzy. Callahan assured me that such fuzziness is normal with infrared film. It was a good indication, he said, that the rest of the processing would be successful. As it turned out, every one of our seventy-five photographs developed perfectly.

Not before he had spent two months in examination and evaluation of the photographs was my friend ready to release his preliminary findings to the press, cautioning even then that final conclusions might well be years in the future. The most important of his findings—and the primary aim of our examination—regarded the presence or absence of an undersketch. While the absence of a preliminary sketch is not incontrovertible proof that the Guadalupe is miraculous, the *presence* of such a sketch would have proved once and for all that an earthly artist had created the painting.

The practice of making a rough sketch before proceeding with a portrait traces back to antiquity. In the Apocryphal Acts of John, which date to the second century A.D., it is related that the artist took two days to paint a portrait of the apostle, spending the entire first day drawing a true-to-life sketch. Only when he was satisfied with the sketch did the artist take up his paintbrush.

Dr. Callahan examined the closeup infrared photographs of the fold shadows of the robe and mantle. He writes:

The fold shadows of the robe may, under cursory examination, appear to be thin sketch lines. However, closeups of both the robe and the mantle show them to be broad, and also *blended with the paint* and, therefore, uncharacteristic of undersketching . . . as in the case of the blue mantle, the shadowing of the pink robe is blended into the paint layer, and no drawing or sketch is evident under the pink pigment.

The closeups of the Virgin's hands led to the same conclusion:

The . . . hands, as in the case of the robe and mantle, show no undersketching whatever. The shading, coloring, and pigments of the . . . hands are inexplicable.

Some thin black lines, which outline the entire left side of the figure from the shoulder downward, might seem to provide a sort of preliminary guide for the painting of the body, but the fact is that these black lines were applied some time after the blue of the mantle but before the gold border had been added. Dr. Callahan reports:

Since the black is opaque to the infrared, the border outline shows up much better than it does in the visible [light] photographs where it is obscured by the shadows of the mantle . . . the added black outline trim often misses the incorporated shadow . . . around the edge . . . a careless job of outlining for Gothic emphasis.

Finally Dr. Callahan examined closeups of the beautifully serene face of the Virgin. Of all parts of the painting, undersketching was most likely to be found here. He found none.

The eyes and shadows around the nose are simple dark
lines that are not underdrawn but are, rather, part of the
face pigment . . . [the face] does not show an un-
derdrawing or sizing of any type . . . These are characteristics which, of themselves, render the painting fantas-
tic.

Examination of the infrared photographs led to another
important discovery—the existence of four fold-marks at
about the level of the Virgin's hands.

"Two of the four fold-lines," observes Dr. Callahan,
"are easily visible across the Virgin's body. The two top
fold-lines cross the entire body but *end at the edge of the
mantle*. They also cross the tassel at the center of the
painting. They do not appear at all across the sunburst, or
any part of the background surrounding the body of the
figure."

From his unprecedented discovery of these folds, Callahan was able to deduce when certain additions had
been made on the original painting. In particular, he observes that "the background was added after the rest of
the painting was formed." Had the background been
present when the Image was folded (perhaps when the
painting was moved during the floods that inundated
Mexico City about 1630), it would have shown the same
fold-marks as are apparent on the body of the Virgin.

In addition to the background, the black outlines, the
gold rays, and the gold trim and stars on the mantle and
fleur-de-lis on the robe, it is generally agreed that the entire bottom third of the painting is a later addition.

"The cherub," says Callahan, "is at best a mediocre

drawing. The arms are clumsy and out of proportion and obviously added to support the Virgin Mary. The face is lifelike, but has none of the beauty or genius of technique shown in the elegant face of the Virgin . . . the hair is probably black oxide of iron. It *overlaps* the moon, as shown by the drawn line which circumscribes it . . . the red of the angel's robe, unlike the Virgin's delicately colored . . . is laid on thickly and is completely opaque to the infrared, indicating that it is in all probability red oxide, an extremely permanent pigment, yet chipping at its outer edges."

The wing feathers seem to be of the same form of red. The wing blue is "badly cracked [and] probably a form of copper-oxide 'Mayan Blue,' laid on, like the thick black of the moon, so thickly as to be subject to heavy cracking."

Callahan concludes that "the angel was added after the moon" because of the overlapping of the angel's hair. This part of the painting, he notes, is "in an extremely bad state of repair." The same black appears on the brooch at the neck of the Virgin and in the hair of the cherub. Like the gold leaf of the rays, it is completely opaque to the infrared, indicating a metallic base to the paint.

Callahan suggests three possibilities: silver nitrate, carbon black, and iron oxide (slate black is too gray). Carbon black, which did not come into use until 1884, must be excluded, since these additions to the original painting had clearly been made, on the evidence of extant copies, by the seventeenth century. While Callahan emphasizes that no certain identification of color composition can be made without chemical analysis, he favors iron oxide: "chemically ferric oxide . . . known by painters as Mars Black . . . [it] is a dense, opaque, permanent color almost brownish in undertones." It also has a tendency to turn browner with time. "Since it is a heavy pigment," Callahan adds, "it would be expected to crack away with age if not properly bound to the canvas." Both browning and cracks are visible in the bottom third of the painting.

The bottom fold of the Virgin's robe presents another curiosity. The same distinctive fold can be seen in other famous paintings of the sixteenth century in America, in particular, *The Tribute Roll of Montezuma*. In that picture hundreds of Aztecs are shown presenting their tilmas as gifts to their new rulers, the Spaniards. Brightly colored, each of the tilmas shows a consistent and apparently symbolic shape. It involves the folds placed diagonally on opposing corners of the tilma. Callahan calls it the "Aztec tilma-fold."

Whatever its purpose for the Aztecs, it was added to the bottom of the Guadalupe. "The simple fact," Dr. Callahan notes, "is that some artist (not a very good one) went to great pains to duplicate the tilma-fold at the base of the Virgin's robe." The tilma-fold was, like the cherub, put on after the crescent moon because "between the line and the visible black moon, one half of the moon was brushed over by the lower edge of the robe and (in infrared) shows through it." There is a "poorly drawn black line which folds into the base of the robe. The same black line was drawn above the foot, but is cracked off.

Both the posterior portion of the foot and the moon lie *under* this segment of the . . . fold, but barely show through because of the opaque (even to infrared) paint of the moon."

Every artist who has ever examined the painting, from 1666 onward, has remarked on the apparent absence of sizing. But they are only partially correct. The bottom third of the Image we found to be clearly if clumsily sized by the layered application of paint to the originally unsized surface. Moreover, brushstrokes, so notably absent from the original parts of the painting, can readily be seen here. The blue color of the tilma-fold is not of the same composition as the blue of the Virgin's mantle. The turquoise blue of the mantle is radically and strangely different.

"The mantle," Callahan reports, "is of a dark turquoise blue, more toward a blue than a green hue. It does *not* appear to be what artists call turquoise green (cobalt oxides mixed with chromium and aluminum). It is also unlikely to be Bremen or Lime blue (mixtures of copper hydroxide carbonate). [Although] Bremen/Lime Blue can be mixed to a great number of shades of blue or greenish blue . . . the mantle shade is (closer) to the hue seen on early Mayan wall-paintings, or on the cured animal-skin 'books' of the Mixtecs. These colors are likely to have been made from copper oxide." But, says Callahan, "this presents an inexplicable phenomenon, because all such blues are semi-permanent and known to be subject to considerable fading with time, especially in hot climates." The blue of the mantle, Callahan observes, "is of even density and not faded . . . of unknown, semi-transparent blue pigment . . . bright enough to have been laid on last week."

Callahan finds the rose-pink of the robe even more mysterious than the blue of the mantle. "The robe is highly reflective of visible radiation, yet transparent to the infrared rays . . . of all the pigments studied, the rose is by far the most transparent . . . it is unlikely to be either cinnabar or heratite, both of which are Indian red pigments; nor is it orange mineral (too yellowish), as all of these minerals are opaque and not transparent to infrared rays. Red lead may be excluded for the same reason. Red oxide is an absolutely permanent pigment . . . it would be a likely candidate, except that it is also extremely opaque to infrared rays. This leaves little but the modern aniline reds. [Yet] there is no evidence anywhere in this painting of any modern aniline colors . . . it appears to be inexplicable."

Also inexplicable is the black of the Virgin's hair. Unlike the brownish black of later additions to the painting, "The black of the hair," Callahan writes, "cannot be iron oxide or any other pigment that turns brown with age, for the paint is neither cracked nor faded."

But perhaps the most amazing part of the painting is the Virgin's face. I have already mentioned how the color of the face seems to change when viewed from different angles because of the diffraction of light from the rough threads of the cactus cloth. This explanation aside, the question of what substances were used to color the face has been a source of unending controversy. Coley Taylor,

New York journalist who co-authored a book entitled *The Dark Virgin*, published in 1956, believes some sort of "wash" or "dye" was used. Dr. Eduardo Turati, an ophthalmologist who studied the "human bust" phenomenon of the eyes in 1975, suggests that the colors were in the original threads before they were woven into cloth. Others have theorized that the original parts of the painting, including the face, were stamped on the cloth in some fashion.

When Dr. Callahan and I viewed the face through a magnifying glass on the night of May 7, 1979, we realized that no one explanation could cover all its mysterious properties. Later, on examining the infrared closeup photographs of the face, Dr. Callahan found the cheek highlight of special interest. It was produced, he reports, from "an unknown white pigment that is practically 'caked on' the coarse fabric. At first glance, it would seem to be blurred in infrared, and then semi-transparent to that radiation . . ." Furthermore:

> If the cheek layers were lime or gypsum, it is almost certain that such an extremely thick application would have cracked over the centuries.

> The pensive-meditative expression, beautiful to behold, is formed by the simple, narrow dark lines that make up the eyebrow, ridge of nose, and mouth . . . close up, the face appears almost devoid of depth . . . but from afar, there is an elegant depth of expression.

> . . . The painting . . . takes advantage of the unsized tilma to give it depth, and render it lifelike. This is par-

ticularly evident in the mouth . . . where a coarse fiber of the fabric is raised above the level of the rest of the weave, and follows perfectly the ridge of the top of the lip. The same rough imperfections occur below the highlighted area on the left cheek, and below the right eye.

Dr. Callahan concludes:

I would consider it impossible that any human painter could select a tilma with imperfections of weave positioned as to accentuate the shadows and highlights so to impart such realism. The possibility of coincidence is even more unlikely!

In this he agrees with the many millions who, over the centuries, have decided that the beautiful face of the Virgin is, pure and simply, miraculous. No amount of scientific analysis can account for the overall effect of the painting. Both Dr. Callahan and I were forced to admit that, in some irreducible way, the Image of Guadalupe is indeed a miracle.

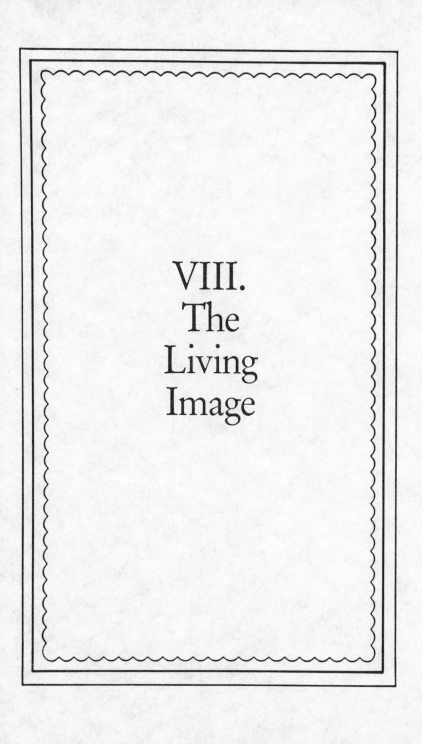

VIII.
The
Living
Image

> I started to wonder what would happen if the cosmos were not a desert and its beauty not a mask or deception . . . then suddenly a wonderful encounter took place in Dresden . . . The eyes of the Heavenly Queen . . . pierced my soul. I cried joyful and yet bitter tears, and with them the ice melted from my soul.
>
> Sergius Bulgakov, on first seeing Raphael's Sistine Madonna

SOME MAY FIND IT IRONIC THAT IN OUR SKEPTICAL AGE the tools of science have been used not to disprove but in some degree to authenticate miracles of the past. Our discovery of the absence of undersketching in the Guadalupe and our inability to account for the remarkable state of preservation of the unsized cactus cloth as well as the unfading brightness of the paints or dyes used in the original parts of the painting put Dr. Callahan and myself firmly in the ranks of those who believe the Image was created supernaturally.

What we saw during those four hours that we examined and photographed the picture in the vault of the basilica on May 7, 1979, also strengthened our conviction that further research, while incapable of solving the essential mystery of the Guadalupe's creation, could greatly

enrich our understanding of the picture. Accordingly, on
June 17, 1979, I wrote Monseñor Enrique Salazar as follows:

> We would like to request of you, Mons. Salazar and
> Abbot Schulenburg-Prado, the opportunity to do some
> further photography and other research, i.e., ultraviolet
> photos; far-infrared spectroscopy and Fourier analysis—
> this requires computerization, but can in many cases de-
> termine the atomic and molecular nature of the colors
> . . . It is precisely this area which is the basis of Dr.
> Callahan's worldwide reputation. Further studies (. . .
> over a period of years more probably than months)
> would be radiographic and/or X-ray fluorescence analy-
> sis; perhaps carbon-14 analysis; ideally, ion microprobe
> analysis, sometime.
>
> What we propose as a logical next step, *because the in-*
> *frared photos show neither an underdrawing of the face*
> *of the Sacred Image, nor any evidence of brushstrokes*
> *thereon,* is to try to ascertain the chemical nature of the
> colors. One or more of the methods outlined above may
> be able to do this . . . (italics added)

After further correspondence with Monseñor Salazar
and with Monseñor Maurilio Montemayor, secretary of the
Center for Guadalupan Studies, whose encouragement of
our research was invaluable, we were able to arrange a
second viewing of the painting in April 1981. At that time
we were able to accomplish something of the eight
specific procedures requested by Dr. Callahan that I had
described to Abbot Schulenburg in a letter the preceding
September:

1) 20 near-ultraviolet photographs of the front of the tilma
2) 20 near-ultraviolet photographs of the back of the tilma
3) 20 near-infrared closeup photographs of the back of the tilma
4) 20 (computer enhancement type) black and white photographs of the tilma back
5) 20 additional near-infrared closeup photographs of the "fold-lines" of the obverse side of the tilma, including any pulled threads or such areas where the cloth might seem to be damaged . . .
6) One small fiber from the edge of the tilma, for a laboratory (spectroscopic; electron-microscopic) study of its composition.
7) The collection of any particulate matter (probably microscopic) from the *Imagen*, by means of gentle application of specially prepared small cloths . . .
8) The co-incident exposure of special-grade color photographs of the two sides of the *Imagen*.

Ultimately, spectrophotometry of the painting was done by Donald J. Lynn, a scientist associated with the Jet Propulsion Laboratory in Pasadena, California. As of this writing, results of this procedure have not been reported.

The nature of further research will depend on what is learned from the April 1981 session.

Meanwhile, based on what we have discovered so far and on my own continuing historical studies, certain suspicions regarding the painting can be laid firmly to rest. For example, to account for the brightness of the colors in mantle and robe, many people have suspected that artists employed by the Church have, from time to time, in the last four hundred and fifty years, been called in to retouch the portrait. But in the original portions of the painting there is absolutely no sign of retouching—no brushstrokes, no cracked or chipped pigment, no layering of paint. In short, the unfading brightness of the turquoise and rose colors remains inexplicable.

Did a human artist paint the portrait—perhaps the Aztec artist Marcos Cipac mentioned in the first official inquiry of 1556? If he did, he did so without making a preliminary sketch—in itself a near-miraculous procedure. My own theory is that Cipac may well have had a hand in painting the Image, but only in painting the additions, such as the angel and moon at the Virgin's feet. How the life-sized figure of the Virgin was imposed on the rough cloth of a peasant's cape in the first place remains mysterious. Even if at some later date we determine that it was stamped, dyed, or woven into the fabric, we are scarcely closer to solving the mystery.

In the four years since I first stood in a line of worshippers to view the Virgin of Guadalupe, my fascination with the miraculous Image has steadily deepened. While scientific and historical research will answer some of the many remaining questions surrounding the painting, the essential mystery of Guadalupe—her hold on millions of Christians over the centuries—is irreducible.

Epilogue

MUCH HAS BEEN HAPPENING AS A RESULT OF SCIENTIFIC RE-search surrounding the Image of Guadalupe and since the rest of this book was written, new facts have come to light regarding, first, the images in the eye of the Virgin and, second and more dramatic, a topic that only now is sufficiently clarified to be reported—the physical examination of the colors and fabrics of the tilma itself.

The enigma of the eye[1] reviewed the discovery of a "human bust" by Marcué, Salinas, and consequently by several ophthalmologists in the 1950s and early '70s. Brief mention was made before of the new work in this field being undertaken by a computer expert named Aste.

Dr. José Aste-Tonsmann has recently completed research begun in early 1979. His study was independent of my own begun late in 1978 and thus each constitutes a valuable reinforcement of the other. Dr. Aste generously shared with me his procedures and conclusions during my January 1982 visit to his Mexico City home and the account here is drawn from his work. While it is beyond the scope of this book to comprehensively detail his research,[2]

[1] See chapter VI.
[2] Aste-Tonsmann, José, Ph.D., *Los Ojos de la Virgen de Guadalupe*. Mexico City: Editorial Diana, October 1981. Highly recommended to readers of Spanish; incorporates and exceeds this pres-

a brief survey of his achievements and the astonishing results would make a most interesting addition to this study.

Dr. Aste's computer has reproduced an enhanced view
of the tilma, with attention being given to sections as
small as 6/1,000,000 meter. He has concentrated attention on the eyes of the Virgin through a process called
digitalization. This photo-enhancing involved the assign-
ment of numerical equivalents to originally qualitative
values. The resulting printout allows us to evaluate images too small to interpret visually.

Aste studied *both* eyes in microscopic detail. Before
this, although the suggestion of human shapes has been
discerned in the left eye, most attention had been focused
on the right eye. This right eye contains an obvious
"human bust" observed before the advent of computer
technology. Now, the enhancement has revealed unan-
ticipated detail in *both* eyes. Because of this research,
weight has been added to the argument that the shapes
are genuine images. If what is captured in the eyes is
some kind of visual record, it is logical to assume that the
"human bust" in the right eye, located slightly off center,
will have a corresponding image in the left eye.

The bust in the right eye, as seen from the position of
observer, is in the upper left quadrant of the pupil. That
image in the left eye was located by Dr. Aste in the
"upper center." This slight difference in position would
be acceptable because of the lateral distance between the
eyes in the human face.

___

ent summary, and includes further technical data. The material
here (pp. 111–116) is used by kind permission of Dr. Aste.

Perhaps the most startling thing revealed in this contemporary analysis is the questioning of the identity of
the dominant feature in the eye as being the Aztec Juan
Diego. Almost immediately after its announced discovery, this anomaly was made to correspond in the popular
piety with the recipient of the apparition. Indicative of
his high scholarship generally, Aste disclaims the connection by noting that the Aztecs of the time are known to
have been clean-shaven. The dominant "human bust"
clearly provides the shape of a full beard extending down
from the chin.

From the larger perspective, however, the issue is not
who the face-shape represents, but *what* it is, and consequently what it implies about the Image of Guadalupe.

It will be remembered that in the work of Dr. Torija
great emphasis was placed on the apparent conformity of
the bust in the right eye with the Purkinje-Sanson optical
law; that Torija perceived not one but three images of
the same figure in geometrically proper alignment. Does
Dr. Aste's work substantiate this original hypothesis, also
supported by other ophthalmologists? Yes, it does. Pointing to a page in his own book for added emphasis, he told
me that the computer "had corroborated with sufficient
clarity" these internal images, just where they would
have to be if explicable as Purkinje-Sanson phenomenon.

The computer engineer calls the dominant image not
"Juan Diego" but, instead, "a bearded Spaniard." He
readily notes that it is much clearer in the right than in
the left eye, but adds something in terms of the enhancement which was invisible to the naked eye of all previ-

ous observers. Connected to the beard is a shape that
could be the right hand of the figure, perhaps pensively
stroking his beard, as he contemplates the portrait now
emblazoned on the inside of the flower-filled apron.

The new examination finds an image of the "bearded
Spaniard" in both eyes of the painting, and has indicated
the proper locations. We have spoken in some detail
about the right-eye image. Why was the image of the
left-eye "Spaniard" not see for what it was at an earlier
date? Aste's modest answer is also reiteration of the
significance of the remarkable, new study: it is a matter
of magnification. A vague figure was observed but not
discerned with sufficient clarity before the computer was
employed to simultaneously amplify and enhance the
shape.

Other quasi-human shapes are reported by Aste to exist
in both eyes of the painting. Of particular note is a face
in the pupils which, like the "bearded Spaniard," is
clearly reminiscent of human anatomy. It reveals a
bearded, balding head, and the beard is longer and is
pointed, both features different from that of the former
human torso. Having obtained a painting by the famous
Guadalupan artist Miguel Cabrera which portrays Bishop
Juan de Zumárraga, Aste is able to show a certain resem-
blance between the two profiles. Cabrera lived some two
centuries after the event in question, but it is quite possible that he had as a model an accurate portrait of the
Mexican prelate.

This "Zumárraga-form" is perseivable in, as was said,
the pupils of both eyes. The difference is that the indis-

tinct shape is in the right eye, rather than the left, as with the "bearded Spaniard," so the description provided by Aste for the left eye is necessarily more nearly complete than for the right. But if, as he has said, the discovery of the major bust in the left eye was a function of the greater magnification or resolution available via computer, one might wonder why the same would not apply to the "Zumárraga" in the eye so intensely studied in the past.

The contribution of the computer is not exclusively one of literal enhancement or even clarification through magnification. As important as these functions can be, there is another property of this process which in the present research is of far greater importance. It is associated with a technique known to mathematicians as "statistical mapping." What is ultimately so impressive about Dr. Aste's work is not the perceivable facial shapes; if it were, we might well be studying a modified Rorschach ink blot. Rather, what impresses the qualified observer is that these several anomalies are positioned in the corresponding eyes in such a fashion as to be virtually beyond coincidence.

A random accumulation of pigments, some of which seem to resemble known forms, is interesting but subject to wide interpretation. In the case at hand, the shapes are positioned at *precisely* the locations demanded by optical geometry and therefore cannot be dismissed.

Nor are these the only shapes discovered and aligned in the respective eyes in the new research. Also discerned is a cluster of forms (Aste calls this the "indigenous family group") and, even further, a seated figure. This figure appears to have the right leg drawn up in front and the left leg extended parallel to the floor. This "seated Indian" appears to be female, and quite large, having a total length of more than four millimeters. The Peruvian researcher observed in our conversation that though he had studied this one shape for over a year, he was still learning new things about it, and about other mysterious forms by means of comparison to it.

While visiting the Basilica of the Virgin of Guadalupe to obtain permission for scientific study, just before Christmas 1978, I was presented with a book, a gift from Monseñor Enrique Salazar. It was the reason for my subsequent meeting with its co-author, Carlos Salinas (the other, Manuel de la Mora, contributed to the work of José Aste), and with Dr. Torija. But it provided the stimulus for still another related quest which I have not mentioned in the body of this work.

Salinas and De la Mora's book[3] was not exclusively devoted to the mystery of the Guadalupan eyes. One section of the book noted that, at one time, fibers from the original had somehow been obtained and ultimately submitted to chemical testing. One of these tests resulted in the exact classification of the cloth, confirming it to be indeed ayate or maguey cactus. Moreover, even its subspecies (*Zacc.*) was identified.

But there was a claim that another test had been done.

[3.] *Discovery of a Human Bust in the Eyes of the Virgin of Guadalupe* (Mexico City: Editorial Tradición, 1976).

The reported results, if valid, were electrifying. In the secondary source was a detailed description of how a yellow and a red thread of the tilma had been hand-carried from Mexico by one of the small group of organic chemists of that era to the laboratory of his own former professor in Germany. A microchemical analysis of the two fibers was unable to ascertain the nature of the dyes or coloring agents used. The only record of the results of the tests was the rather cryptic pronouncement that they were "neither animal, vegetable, or mineral," i.e., neither organic nor inorganic. Mr. Salinas' work called attention to the fact that *synthetic* colors were not formulated until after 1850, thereby excluding the only other obvious solution.

What I needed to know were the details. I needed the original, the primary sources, exactly what procedures had been utilized. From exactly what part of the relic had the two fibers been obtained? What were the details behind the terse announced results?

Many obstacles imposed themselves during the more than three years since I began my efforts, notwithstanding the efforts of many friends, both Mexican and German. Communication, via the scientific attaché of the Embassy of the Federal Republic of Germany with the son of the Nobel Laureate ostensibly connected with the 1936 research, produced no records. Consequently, I thought the problem lacking any immediate solution.

What I had sought, from the beginning, was some sort of physical sample to test with contemporary tools, such as the electron microscope. Until a test sample was made available, we wanted to assemble a complete file on the previous experiment, so that record, fragmentary though it was, could be compared with any work we might eventually do.

Had the experiments really been done? What tools, equipment, methods were applied? Were the conclusions subjected to corroboration? Had they been destroyed in World War II? Did anybody, anywhere, have the primary materials, or, if not, a reasonable facsimile thereof?

On hearsay evidence, the documents and perhaps even the tested fibers themselves still survive. But each has been secreted away, and the chances of ever perusing either appear to decline with each passing month.

Though there undoubtedly will be more developments in updating our knowledge of the Guadalupan Image— perhaps even in the area mentioned above—I have thought it best to publish the present findings now. (*JBS*, 1982)

Since the first edition of this book was published, the unexpected has happened: a tiny piece of material from the Guadalupe tilma came into my possession. The process of obtaining this piece—which appears to have been secured almost fifty years ago—required five years of patience. Although its source must remain confidential, thanks are hereby extended to the gracious donor.

At the present time, only a limited amount of further investigation has been accomplished. This work is centered around the successful microphotography of the tiny filament from the tilma, included here as photograph 23. Eventual chemical analysis of the fiber is anticipated.

Appendices

The Nican Mopohua[1]

The nican mopohua—Nahuatl for "an account"—is the most complete and probably the earliest written record of the legend of Juan Diego. For many years it was believed to be a concoction of the seventeenth century when interest in anything relating to the Virgin of Guadalupe was at an all-time high. The name of the reputed Indian author, Antonio Valeriano, was thought to be a pseudonym, since no independent proof of Valeriano's existence could be found.

The recent discovery of a sixteenth-century civil paper signed by "Antonio Valeriano" confirmed his existence and also helped to establish that the nican mopohua was composed in the sixteenth century. Most scholars now believe that the nican mopohua was written sometime between 1551 and 1561, twenty to thirty years after the mi-

[1.] Translated from the Spanish by Cleofas Callero, M.F.A., in *Am I Not Here?* by Harold J. Rahm, S.J., Washington, N.J., 1961. This work is originally from *Álbum Histórico Guadalupano del IV Centenario* by P. Mariano Cuevas, S.J. Escuela Tipográfica Salesiana, Mexico, D.F., 1930, Tercera Decada—1551–1561.

raculous happenings on Tepeyac hill and in the bishop's palace.

TEN YEARS AFTER THE SEIZURE OF THE CITY OF MEXICO, WAR came to an end and there was peace amongst the people; in this manner faith started to bud, the understanding of the true God, for whom we live. At that time, in the year fifteen hundred and thirty-one, in the early days of the month of December, it happened that there lived a poor Indian, named Juan Diego, said being a native of Cuautitlán. Of all things spiritually he belonged to Tlatilolco. On a Saturday just before dawn, he was on his way to pursue divine worship and to engage in his own errands. (As he reached) the base of the hill known as Tepeyacac, came the break of day, and he heard singing atop the hill, resembling singing of varied beautiful birds. Occasionally the voices of the songsters would cease, and it appeared as if the mount responded. The song, very mellow and delightful, excelled that of the *coyoltototl* and the *tziniz-can*[2] and of other pretty singing birds. Juan Diego stopped to look and said to himself: "By fortune, am I worthy of what I hear? Maybe I dream? Am I awakening? Where am I? Perhaps I am in the terrestrial paradise which our elders had told us about? Perhaps I am now in heaven?" He was looking toward the east, on top of the mound, from whence came the precious celestial chant; and then it suddenly ceased and there was silence. He

[2.] Nahuatl names for two varieties of birds for which there are no English equivalents.

then heard a voice from above the mound saying to him: *"Juanito, Juan Dieguito."* Then he ventured and went to where he was called. He was not frightened in the least; on the contrary, overjoyed. Then he climbed the hill, to see from where he was being called. When he reached the summit, he saw a Lady, who was standing there and who told him to come hither. Approaching her presence, he marveled greatly at her superhuman grandeur; her garments were shining like the sun; the cliff where she rested her feet, pierced with glitter, resembling an anklet of precious stones, and the earth sparkled like the rainbow. The *mezquites, nopales,* and other different weeds, which grow there, appeared like emeralds, their foliage like turquoise, and their branches and thorns glistened like gold. He bowed before her and heard her word, tender and courteous, like someone who charms and esteems you highly. She said: *"Juanito,* the most humble of my sons, where are you going?" He replied: "My Lady and Child, I have to reach your church in Mexico, Tlatilolco, to pursue things divine, taught and given to us by our priests, delegates, and Our Lord." She then spoke to him, revealing her holy will. She told him: "Know and understand well, you the most humble of my sons, that I am the ever-virgin Holy Mary, Mother of the True God for whom we live, of the Creator of all things, Lord of heaven and the earth. I wish that a temple be erected here quickly, so I may therein exhibit and give all my love, compassion, help, and protection, because I am your merciful mother, to you, and to all the inhabitants on this earth and all the rest who love me, invoke and confide in

me; listen there to their lamentations, and remedy all
their miseries, afflictions, and sorrows. And to accomplish
what my clemency pretends, go to the palace of the
bishop of Mexico, and you will say to him that I manifest
my great desire, that here on the plain a temple be built
to me; you will accurately relate all you have seen and
admired, and what you have heard. Be assured that I will
be most grateful and will reward you, because I will
make you happy and worthy of recompense for the effort
and fatigue in what you will obtain of what I have en-
trusted. Behold, you have heard my mandate, my humble
son; go and put forth all your effort." At this point he
bowed before her and said: "My Lady, I am going to
comply with your mandate; now I must part from you, I,
your humble servant." Then he descended to go to comply with the errand, and went by the avenue which runs
directly into Mexico City.

Having entered the city, and without delay, he went
straight to the bishop's palace, who was the recently arrived prelate named Father Juan de Zumárraga, a Franciscan religious. On arrival, he endeavored to see him; he
pleaded with the servants to announce him; and after a
long wait, he was called and advised that the bishop had
ordered his admission. As he entered, he bowed, and on
bended knees before him, he then delivered the message
from the Lady from heaven; he also told him all he had
admired, seen, and heard. After having heard his chat
and message, it appeared incredible; then he told him:
"You will return, my son, and I will hear you at my pleasure. I will review it from the beginning and will give

thought to the wishes and desires for which you have come." He left and he seemed sad, because his message had not been realized in any of its forms.

He returned on the same day. He came directly to the top of the hill, met the Lady from heaven, who was awaiting him, in the same spot where he saw her the first time. Seeing her, prostrated before her, he said: "Lady, the least of my daughters, my Child, I went where you sent me to comply with your command. With difficulty I entered the prelate's study. I saw him and exposed your message, just as you instructed me. He received me benevolently and listened attentively, but when he replied, it appeared that he did not believe me. He said: 'You will return; I will hear you at my pleasure. I will review from the beginning the wish and desire which you have brought.' I perfectly understood by the manner he replied that he believes it to be an invention of mine that you wish that a temple be built here to you, and that it is not your order; for which I exceedingly beg, Lady and my Child, that you entrust the delivery of your message to someone of importance, well known, respected, and esteemed, so that they may believe in him; because I am a nobody, I am a small rope, a tiny ladder, the tail end, a leaf, and you, my Child, the least of my children, my Lady, you send me to a place where I never visit nor repose. Please excuse the great unpleasantness and let not fretfulness befall, my Lady and my All." The Blessed Virgin answered: "Hark, my son the least, you must understand that I have many servants and messengers, to whom I can entrust the delivery of my message, and

carry my wish, but it is of precise detail that you yourself
solicit and assist and that through your mediation my
wish be complied. I earnestly implore, my son the least,
and with sternness I command that you again go tomorrow and see the bishop. You go in my name, and make
known my wish in its entirety that he has to start the
erection of a temple which I ask of him. And again tell
him that I, in person, the ever-virgin Holy Mary, Mother
of God, send you." Juan Diego replied: "Lady, my Child,
let me not cause you affliction. Gladly and willingly I will
go to comply your mandate. Under no condition will I
fail to do it, for not even the way is distressing. I will go
to do your wish, but perhaps I will not be heard with lik-
ing, or if I am heard I might not be believed. Tomorrow
afternoon, at sunset, I will come to bring you the result of
your message with the prelate's reply. I now take leave,
my Child, the least, my Child and Lady. Rest in the
meantime." He then left to rest in his home.

The next day, Sunday, before dawn, he left home on his
way to Tlatilolco, to be instructed in things divine, and to
be present for roll call, following which he had to see the
prelate. Nearly at ten, and swiftly, after hearing Mass and
being counted and the crowd had dispersed, he went. On
the hour Juan Diego left for the palace of the bishop.
Hardly had he arrived, he eagerly tried to see him. Again
with much difficulty he was able to see him. He kneeled
before his feet. He saddened and cried as he expounded
the mandate of the Lady from heaven, which God grant
he would believe his message, and the wish of the Im-
maculate, to erect her temple where she willed it to be.

The bishop, to assure himself, asked many things, where
he had seen her and how she looked; and he described
everything perfectly to the bishop. Notwithstanding his
precise explanation of her figure and all that he had seen
and admired, which in itself reflected her as being the
ever-virgin Holy Mother of the Saviour, Our Lord Jesus
Christ, nevertheless, he did not give credence and said
that not only for his request he had to do what he had
asked; that, in addition, a sign was very necessary, so that
he could be believed that he was sent by the true Lady
from heaven. Therefore, he was heard, said Juan Diego to
the bishop: "My lord, hark! what must be the sign that
you ask? For I will go to ask the Lady from heaven who
sent me here." The bishop, seeing that he ratified everything without doubt and (was) not retracting anything,
dismissed him. Immediately he ordered some persons of
his household, in whom he could trust, to go and watch
where he went and whom he saw and to whom he spoke.
So it was done. Juan Diego went straight to the avenue.
Those that followed him, as they crossed the ravine, near
the bridge to Tepeyacac, lost sight of him. They searched
everywhere, but he could not be seen. Thus they returned, not only because they were disgusted, but also
because they were hindered in their intent, causing them
anger. And that is what they informed the bishop,
influencing him not to believe Juan Diego; they told him
that he was being deceived; that Juan Diego was only
forging what he was saying, or that he was simply dream-
ing what he said and asked. They finally schemed that if

he ever returned, they would hold and punish him harshly, so that he would never lie or deceive again.

In the meantime, Juan Diego was with the Blessed Virgin, relating the answer he was bringing from his lordship, the bishop. The Lady, having heard, told him: "Well and good, my little dear, you will return here tomorrow, so you may take to the bishop the sign he has requested. With this he will believe you, and in this regard he will not doubt you nor will he be suspicious of you; and know, my little dear, that I will reward your solicitude and effort and fatigue spent on my behalf. Lo! go now. I will await you here tomorrow."

On the following day, Monday, when Juan Diego was to carry a sign so he could be believed, he failed to return, because, when he reached his home, his uncle, named Juan Bernardino, had become sick, and was gravely ill. First he summoned a doctor who aided him; but it was too late, he was gravely ill. By nightfall, his uncle requested that by break of day he go to Tlatilolco and summon a priest, to prepare him and hear his confession, because he was certain that it was time for him to die, and that he would not arise or get well.

On Tuesday, before dawn, Juan Diego came from his home to Tlatilolco to summon a priest; and as he approached the road which joins the slope to Tepeyacac hilltop, toward the west, where he was accustomed to cross, said: "If I proceed forward, the Lady is bound to see me, and I may be detained, so I may take the sign to the prelate, as prearranged; that our first affliction must let us go hurriedly to call a priest, as my poor uncle cer-

tainly awaits him." Then he rounded the hill, going
around, so he could not be seen by her who sees well everywhere. He saw her descend from the top of the hill
and was looking toward where they previously met. She
approached him at the side of the hill and said to him:
"What's there, my son the least? Where are you going?"
Was he grieved, or ashamed, or scared? He bowed before
her. He saluted, saying: "My Child, the most tender of
my daughters, Lady, God grant you are content. How are
you this morning? Is your health good, Lady and my
Child? I am going to cause you grief. Know, my Child,
that a servant of yours is very sick, my uncle. He has con-
tracted the plague, and is near death. I am hurrying to
your house in Mexico to call one of your priests, beloved
by our Lord, to hear his confession and absolve him, because, since we were born, we came to guard the work
of our death. But if I go, I shall return here soon, so I may
go to deliver your message. Lady and my Child, forgive
me, be patient with me for the time being. I will not deceive you, the least of my daughters. Tomorrow I will
come in all haste." After hearing Juan Diego's chat, the
Most Holy Virgin answered: "Hear me and understand
well, my son the least, that nothing should frighten or
grieve you. Let not your heart be disturbed. Do not fear
that sickness, nor any other sickness or anguish. Am I not
here, who is your Mother? Are you not under my protection? Am I not your health? Are you not happily within
my fold? What else do you wish? Do not grieve nor be
disturbed by anything. Do not be afflicted by the illness
of your uncle, who will not die now of it. Be assured that

he is now cured." (And then his uncle was cured, as it was later learned.) When Juan Diego heard these words from the Lady from heaven, he was greatly consoled. He was happy. He begged to be excused to be off to see the bishop, to take him the sign or proof, so that he might be believed. The Lady from heaven ordered him to climb to the top of the hill, where they previously met. She told him: "Climb, my son the least, to the top of the hill; there where you saw me and I gave you orders, you will find different flowers. Cut them, gather them, assemble them, then come and bring them before my presence." Immediately Juan Diego climbed the hill, and as he reached the summit, he was amazed that so many varieties of exquisite *rosas de Castilla* were blooming, long before the time when they are to bud, because, being out of season, they would freeze. They were very fragrant and covered with dewdrops of the night, which resembled precious pearls. Immediately he started cutting them. He gathered them all and placed them in his tilma. The hilltop was no place for any kind of flowers to grow, because it had many crags, thistles, thorns, *nopales,* and *mezquites.* Occasionally weeds would grow, but it was then the month of December, in which all vegetation is destroyed by freezing. He immediately went down the hill and brought the different roses which he had cut to the Lady from heaven, who, as she saw them, took them with her hand and again placed them back in the tilma, saying: "My son the least, this diversity of roses is the proof and the sign which you will take to the bishop. You will tell him in my name that he will see in them my wish and that he will have to comply to it. You are my ambassador, most worthy of all confidence. Rigorously I command you that only before the presence of the bishop will you unfold your mantle and disclose what you are carrying. You will relate all and well; you will tell that I ordered you to climb to the hilltop, to go and cut flowers; and all that you saw and admired, so you can induce the prelate to give his support, with the aim that a temple be built and erected as I have asked." After the Lady from heaven had given her advice, he was on his way by the avenue that goes directly to Mexico; being happy and assured of success, carrying with great care what he bore in his tilma, being careful that nothing would slip from his hands, and enjoying the fragrance of the variety of the beautiful flowers.

(When he reached) the bishop's palace, there came to meet him the majordomo and other servants of the prelate. He begged them to tell (the bishop) that he wished to see him, but none were willing, pretending not to hear him, probably because it was too early, or because they already knew him as being of the molesting type, because he was pestering them; and, moreover, they had been advised by their co-workers that they had lost sight of him, when they had followed him. He waited a long time. When they saw that he had been there a long time, standing, crestfallen, doing nothing, waiting to be called, and appearing like he had something which he carried in his tilma, they came near him, to see what he had and to satisfy themselves. Juan Diego, seeing that he could not hide what he had, and on account of that he would be mo-

lested, pushed or mauled, uncovered his tilma a little, and
there were the flowers; and upon seeing that they were
all different *rosas de Castilla,* and out of season, they were
thoroughly amazed, also because they were so fresh and
in full bloom, so fragrant and so beautiful. They tried to
seize and pull some out, but they were not successful
the three times they dared to take them. They were not
lucky because when they tried to get them, they were
unable to see real flowers. Instead, they appeared painted
or stamped or sewn on the cloth. Then they went to tell the
bishop what they had seen and that the Indian who had
come so many times wished to see him, and that he had
reason enough to wait so long anxiously eager to see him.
Upon hearing, the bishop realized that what he carried
was the proof, to confirm and comply with what the Indian requested. Immediately he ordered his admission. As
he entered, Juan Diego knelt before him, as he was accustomed to do, and again related what he had seen and admired, also the message. He said: "Sir, I did what you ordered, to go forth and tell my *Ama,* the Lady from
heaven, Holy Mary, precious Mother of God, that you
asked for a sign so that you might believe me that you
should build a temple where she asked it to be erected;
also, I told her that I had given you my word that I
would bring some sign and proof, which you requested,
of her wish. She condescended to your request and gra-
ciously granted your request, some sign and proof to
complement her wish. Early today she again sent me to
see you; I asked for the sign so you might believe me, as
she had said that she would give it, and she complied.

She sent me to the top of the hill, where I was accustomed to see her, and to cut a variety of *rosas de Castilla*. After I had cut them, I brought them, she took them with her hand and placed them in my cloth, so that I bring them to you and deliver them to you in person. Even though I knew that the hilltop was no place where flowers would grow, because there are many crags, thistles, thorns, *nopales*, and *mezquites*, I still had my doubts. As I approached the top of the hill, I saw that I was in paradise, where there was a great variety of exquisite *rosas de Castilla*, in brilliant dew, which I immediately cut. She had told me that I should bring them to you, and so I do it, so that you may see in them the sign which you asked of me and comply with her wish; also, to make clear the veracity of my word and my message. Behold. Receive them." He then unfolded his white cloth, where he had the flowers; and when they scattered on the floor, all the different varieties of *rosas de Castilla*, suddenly there appeared the drawing of the precious Image of the ever-virgin Holy Mary, Mother of God, in the manner as she is today kept in the temple at Tepeyacac, which is named Guadalupe. When the bishop saw the image, he and all who were present fell to their knees. She was greatly admired. They arose to see her; they shuddered and, with sorrow, they demonstrated that they contemplated her with their hearts and minds. The bishop, with sorrowful tears, prayed and begged forgiveness for not having attended her wish and request. When he rose to his feet, he untied from Juan Diego's neck the cloth on which appeared the Image of the Lady from

heaven. Then he took it to be placed in his chapel. Juan
Diego remained one more day in the bishop's house, at
his request. The following day he told him: "Well! show
us where the Lady from heaven wished her temple be
erected." Immediately, he invited all those present to go.
As Juan Diego pointed out the spot where the Lady from
heaven wanted her temple built, he begged to be excused. He wished to go home to see his uncle Juan Bernardino, who was gravely ill when he left him to go to
Tlatilolco to summon a priest, to hear his confession and
absolve him. The Lady from heaven had told him that he
had been cured. But they did not let him go alone, and
accompanied him to his home. As they arrived, they saw
that his uncle was very happy and nothing ailed him. He
was greatly amazed to see his nephew arrive so accompanied and honored, asking the reason of such honors con-
ferred upon him. His nephew answered that when he left
to summon a priest to hear his confession and to absolve
him, the Lady from heaven appeared to him at Tepeyacac, telling him not to be afflicted, that his uncle was well,
for which he was greatly consoled, and she sent him to
Mexico, to see the bishop, to build her a house in Tepeyacac. Then the uncle manifested that it was true that on
that occasion he became well and that he had seen her in
the same manner as she had appeared to his nephew,
knowing through her that she had sent him to Mexico to
see the bishop. Also, the Lady told him that when he
would go to see the bishop, to reveal to him what he had
seen and to explain the miraculous manner in which she
had cured him, and that she would properly be named,

and known as the blessed Image, the ever-virgin Holy
Mary of Guadalupe. Juan Bernardino was brought before
the presence of the bishop to inform and testify before
him. Both he and his nephew were the guests of the bishop
in his home for some days, until the temple dedicated to
the Queen of Tepeyacac was erected where Juan Diego
had seen her. The bishop transferred the sacred Image of
the lovely Lady from heaven to the main church, taking
her from his private chapel where it was, so that the people would see and admire her blessed Image. The entire
city was aroused; they came to see and admire the devout
Image, and to pray. They marveled at the fact that she
appeared as did her divine miracle, because no living
person of this world had painted her precious Image.

The Primitive Relation

Nahuatl scholar Ángel M. Garibay-Kintana is credited as discoverer of the "Primitive Relation" in the Mexican National Library Archives in the early 1950s. He believed it was written about 1573 by the historian Juan de Tovar, who transcribed it from an earlier source. According to Garibay, the earlier source was Juan González, credited by most Guadalupan historians with being the man who translated Juan Diego's startling message into Spanish in Bishop Zumarraga's palace in 1531. Much fine work has been done since 1976 by Father Mario Rojas of the Center for Guadalupan Studies. The English translation which follows is by Dr. James A. Guest.

Our Lady of Guadalupana

1. This is a great marvel that our Lord God did by means of the forever-virgin Holy Mary.

2. Here it is.

3. That which you should notice, that which you should hear in what miraculous manner it was desired that a house should be erected, that a dwelling should be established, that would be called Queen Holy Mary in Tepeyac.

4. This is what occurred: a poor man of the village, a "macehual" of great piety,

5. said to be laborer (poor creature, poor yokel) there in Tepeyac, was going by walking along the peaks

6. (to see if by chance a little root might have broken through the ground), struggling to earn his living.

7. There he saw the beloved Mother of God, who called him and said to him:

8. "My little son, go to the emperor of the Great City Mexico,

9. SAY TO HIM WHO THERE IS GOVERNING THAT WHICH IS SPIRITUAL, TO THE ARCHBISHOP

10. THAT I WISH WITH A GREAT DESIRE THAT HERE IN TEPEYAC THEY MAKE ME A DWELLING, THAT THEY RAISE UP TO ME MY HOUSE

11. SO THAT HERE THEY COME TO KNOW ME WELL, THAT THE FAITHFUL CHRISTIANS MAY COME HERE TO PRAY TO ME

12. HERE I WILL CONVERT TO ME (IN IT) WHEN THEY MAKE ME THEIR INTERCESSOR."

13. Then that poor little man went to present himself before the great governing priest archbishop, and said to him:

14. "My Lord, I am not going to importune you but, behold, Our Lady of the Heavens has sent me,

15. told me that I should come to say how much she desires that there in Tepeyac should be made, should be erected for her, a house in order that there Christians may supplicate her.

16. She also said to me that something very close to her (in her riches) that there might be converted when they will go there to invoke her."

17. But the archbishop gave him no credit but rather said to him:

18. "What are you saying, my son? Perhaps you have dreamed this or perhaps you have been drunk!

19. If, in truth, it is certain that which you say, (say) to her, to this Lady that said it to you, that she give you any sign

20. In order that we may believe that it is really true what you are saying."

21. He returned, our poor little man, became extremely sad, and there appeared to him again the Queen

22. And when our little man saw her he said to her:

23. "My child, I went whither you did send me, but my lord did not believe me,

24. Moreover he said to me that perhaps I dreamed it or perhaps I had been drunk

25. And he said to me that in order to believe it you should give me a sign in order that it be carried out."

26. And when Our Lady the Queen, the beloved Mother of God, then said to him:

27. "DON'T BE SAD, MY YOUNG ONE, GO TO GATHER, GO CUT SOME LITTLE FLOWERS WHERE THEY ARE BLOOMING."

28. These flowers only by miracle were growing there, because at that season the earth was very dry, no-where were flowers opening.

29. When our little man cut them he put them in the hol-low of his cloak.

30. From there he went to Mexico to tell the bishop:

31. "My Lord, here I bring the flowers that Our Celestial Lady gave me in order that you may believe her word is true, her will, that I have come to tell you, that it is certain that which she said to me."

32. And when he opened his cloak, in order to show the flowers to the archbishop, there also was seen in the cloak of our little man,

33. There was painted, there was converted into a signal portrait the Virgin Queen in prodigious form so that the archbishop believed.

34. On seeing it, they knelt and admired her.

35. And, in truth, the very Image of the Virgin Queen is here only by miracle; in the cloak of the poor man (it) was painted as a portrait, where now (it) is placed as a light for the whole universe.

36. There come to know her those who supplicate her

37. And she, with her pious maternity (with her maternal affection), there helps them, gives them what they ask.

38. And, in truth, if someone fully recognizes by her intermission, and totally gives himself to her, loving her for her intercession, the beloved Mother of God will convert him.

39. In truth, it will help much to her, it will show to her, to whom they esteem (that) they have begun to put themselves under her shadow, under her care.

The Codex Saville

America's Oldest Book[1]

The Codex Saville was found in Tetlapalco in Peru in 1924 by the anthropologist M. H. Saville. It is a pictorial calendar, now in the collection of the Museum of the American Indian in New York City.

The following commentary on the Codex Saville was written by Mariano Cuevas, S.J., who translated the calendar in 1929.

IT HAS ALWAYS BEEN THE PRIVILEGE OF THE FIRST READER OF or commentator on a Codex to give it an appropriate name. It is therefore a pleasant duty for me to designate as the Codex Saville this pre-Columbian Mexican historical paper, now for the first time published under the auspices of the United States Catholic Historical Society. This is the honor due to Doctor Marshall H. Saville whose merits and brilliant successes during the last forty-five years are so much appreciated by students of the ancient history of the Latin-American countries.

The Codex Saville was recently secured in Lima, Peru,

1. From *Historical Records and Studies*, U.S. Catholic Historical Society, N.Y., 1929, vol. XIX, pp. 7–20.

by the Heye Foundation of New York City. It is still only provisionally catalogued.

Its size is 57 × 5 inches (1,45 mts. × 0,26 mts.). It is made of the native *maguey* or *agave* American fibre, conglutinated by a vegetable pulp called in the *nahuatl* or Mexican language *zazalic*. Some linen finished marks that appear here and there on the Codex are only surface clothprints from outside pressure on the paste used at some recent date to put together the separate fragments.

Three small patches of the same native paper were pasted on the main part of the Codex in order, it seems, to correct some dates or data. One of these little papers pasted about the year 1453 is of the utmost importance. Notice that the upper part of it was afterwards scratched out, thus again making visible the original painted sign of the cycle:

similar to the one at the right side of the year 1455.

Originally the Codex was not in colors. These were poorly applied by the painter of the upper and later part some time about 1531.

There were at least two *tecuilos* (painters) of this *amatl* (painting paper). The first one started before 1454; possibly in 1440. The last one, of the remaining part of the Codex, was at his work about 1557. Names of different Mexican towns, most of them now illegible, were written all through the Codex in Spanish characters but with the typical Indian handwriting of the middle of the sixteenth century.

Before commenting on the Codex, I believe that some previous interpretations will be welcomed by readers who are not very familiar either with Codex-reading or with Mexican history and technique.

I. *The Chronology:* The eleborated Chronology of the Nahuatl peoples, inherited, it is said, from the Toltecs, has has been fully illustrated and published by many first-class authors.[2] For the reading of this Codex it is sufficient to bear in mind the main divisions of the time, among the old Mexicans. Their cycle was not of one hundred years but the natural one of fifty-two years. This cycle was divided into four groups each of thirteen years $(4 \times 13 = 52)$. Four different signs were employed to name the years: *tochtli* (rabbit); *acatl* (reed); *tecatl* (stone) and *calli* (house). Each year was named by a combination of one of the above four signs mentioned in succession, together with the corresponding number of the group of thirteen years, named also successively, e.g.: *1, tochtli; 2, acatl; 3, tecatl; 4, calli; 5, tochtli*—and so on until after a period of fifty-two years the same sign occurred again with the same number. The same combination could not occur in the same cycle. A picture of the Codex Aubin shows the cycle as conceived by the Aztecs.

II. *History:* Some time about the end of the twelfth century of our Christian era, seven branches of the race Nahuatl (meaning "clear talking people") were wander-

---

[2.] See Orozco y Berra, *Historia antigua y de la Conquista de México*, Mexico, 1870, vol II, chap. III.

ing at a very slow rate all through the present Mexican Republic. The origin of these people still remains a mystery. With the exception of their very last "pilgrimage" in the region south of the grand plateau of Mexico, the rest of their wanderings are almost lost in the mist of pre-history. One of these seven branches, called *tenochca* and later on *Mexicas* made a final halt (1318) in the center of the present city "because there they saw the unequivocal sign given by the gods: an eagle upon a cactus, devouring a snake."[3]

An older tradition, given as such by a reliable source,[4] was that the sign to stop the wandering of the Mexicans should be a white oak in the middle of the lake.

As soon as the Mexicans made up their minds to remain there, they began to build dikes to protect their swamp dwellings or Venice-like town from the main surrounding lake. Hence the very first name of the city, which, according to Tezozomoc, was not Mexico but *Atl-itc* meaning "water surrounded by a wall." The finishing of that dike, six years later in 1324, was a very good reason to give that date as the foundation of the city. The Codex Saville by giving the date 9 *acatl* (1319) for the end of the pilgrimage, or the beginning of the foundation and *I*

[3.] If it is not a real tradition it is at least the hieroglyphic of what really took place, namely that the *Mexicas* stopped where their explorers bade them. Now, the name of the first explorer was Cuahu-cóatl meaning precisely "eagle with snake" and he was sent and supported by Tenoch meaning precisely "cactus upon the rock." An eagle upon a cactus therefore could be in Mexico a unique and unequivocal sign.
[4.] *Cronica de Mexico* by Don Fernando Alvarado Tezozomoc, written in the sixteenth century. Printed in Mexico, 1898, chap. IX.

tecpal (1324) for the end of the foundation, is the best solution to the endless dispute about that important event.

After the death of the leading warrior Tenoch, of which the date is uncertain, the Mexicans began to "elect" their absolute rulers. Following the Spanish conquerors, although most improperly, we still call them "kings." Their names, as well as the hieroglyphic to represent them, and the corresponding English translations, appear on page 146.

Progress and existence itself became impossible for the *Mexicas,* confined as they were, within their diked swamptown. Meanwhile the Tecpanecas, owners of the lands surrounding the lake, would not give the Mexicans any chance for expansion. The latter, furthermore, were continuously insulted by the powerful Tecpaneca King, Maxtla. He used to call them effeminate people. Mexican ambassadors sent to him by King Itzcóatl in 1432 were again insulted, dressed in women's robes and forced to return in this guise from Tlatilolco to Mexico. No one was thus more humiliated than the head of the embassy, the famous Moctezuma, afterwards Emperor of Mexico.

The rage provoked in the Mexicans by such an outrage finally led to the ferocious war lasting five years. The courage of the Mexicans and the skill of their leaders, Moctezuma and King Itzcóatl, defeated the Tecpanecas. They became masters of the whole grand valley of Mexico and thus had an open door for the conquest of the rest of the country.

Acamaphichtli
Handful of reeds—female snake.

Huitzihuitl
Hummingbird.

Chimalpopoca
Smoking shield.

Itzcóatl
Sword-back serpent

Moctezuma I.
Wrathy-lord

Tizoc
Wounded leg.

Axayacatl
Face in the water.

Ahuizotl
Water rat.

Moctezuma II.
Wrathy-lord

King Itzcóatl, after celebrating his triumph, initiated a series of substantial reformations in the politics of his much enlarged kingdom. A very useful one was the institution of a Council of State to be formed by four prominent noblemen. Out of them the successor for the throne would be selected, thus avoiding the probability of much dangerous competition. This council was instituted during the fifth year of Itzcóatl, A.D. 1437.

Moctezuma I, the next following ruler, carried a victorious war against his powerful Huaxteca neighbors, thus becoming master of the eastern seashore and proving once more that the women's dresses given him by Maxtla were not appropriate.

King Axayacatl was shamefully defeated by Tarasco's brave warriors. Old Mexican historians prefer to forget this unexpected misfortune. They rather turn their eyes to the pompous allies of Mexico, the rich and learned kings of Tezcoco. The most conspicuous of them was Netzahualpilli meaning "hungry child." He was crowned in 1471.

After the short reign of Tizoc the Mexican throne was occupied by Ahuitzotl, one of the most cruel monsters ever seen. The dedication he made of the double temple in 1487, sacrificing more than 20,000 innocent men, stained the history of Mexico forever.

Moctezuma II, crowned in 1502, saw the punishment of such a "civilization" when in 1519 "white men, bearded, silver plated" riding on "big hornless deers" with sword and fire overthrew the Mexican empire.

Nothing from that time could be recorded with pleasure by the *tlacuilos* or history painters. All was pain and disgrace, until in 1526 the Franciscan missionaries, who had arrived two years before, mastered the Nahuatl language and began the evangelization of the country. They started this work by erecting an enormous wooden cross that could be seen for several leagues around, in their churchyard.

Another fact of great importance in Mexican history and Mexican life was the apparition of the Madonna that, according to tradition and reliable documents, took place in 1531 a few miles north of Mexico City, where the present national shrine stands.

All this data about the old Mexican history have been known and printed by many reliable authors long ago and independently of this Codex. In fact no one seems to have even quoted it, lost as it was from the middle of the sixteenth century.

It is fascinating to find records of these main lines in a five-century-old document which is a first-hand work taken directly from contemporary life by eye-witness historians. Of course this book, like all of its age and like many of our own age, would be meaningless without some commentaries. They could only be memoranda, to be commented on by specially trained men called *amo-xoaque*, meaning "men explaining the old paintings."

Reading of the Codex

The series of historical events herein contained was methodically coordinated and framed in the vertical ruler-line, at the right as you read. There we find, reading up, eight groups, each consisting of a corpse and a living man; both are connected with one of the discs in the line indicating a certain year.

From the characteristic hieroglyphic placed upon the heads of most of the figures, we can recognize with certainty the series of the Mexican rulers from 1422 to 1520. It is a most valuable chronological series and may give the last word to what seemed an endless controversy about the dates of the Mexican rulers prior to 1468.

According to the *tlacuilo* of the Codex Saville the succession of the Mexican "kings" was as follows:

Acamapichtli	undated
Huitzihuitl	died 1422
Chimalpopoca	1422–1432
Itzcohuatl or Itzcóatl	1432–1445
Moctezuma I	1455–1467
Axayacatl	1468–1481
Tizoc	1481–1486
Ahuitzotl	1486–1502
Moctezuma II	1502–undated

Cuitlahuac and Cuauhtemoc, emperors for a short time after the conquest, are, of course, not mentioned.

The inside column of the Codex, which is also to be read upwards, has to be divided into two parts: the pre-Cortesian and the post-Cortesian.

A. In the first one we have to consider several groups.
    The arrival of the Mexicans at their final resting
    place is clearly shown by the natural sign of foot-
    prints. Some archaeologists maintain that footprints
    of both feet, in hieroglyphic language, mean the act
    of climbing. If this statement is well founded, so
    much the better for the reading of this part, since
    the last steps of the Mexicans were nothing but
    climbing to the two thousand feet high Mexican
    plateau, where they settled.

B. The majestically enthroned King, as far as we can
    tell, is Acamapichtli. The nickname for the position
    he held at the time of his election) was *chua cóatl*
    (female serpent). Now the woman's face in an ini-
    tiated snake body is just his hieroglyphic expressed
    in this very way by the Codex Mendocino.

C. The oldest name of the City of Mexico. Its white
    oak as well as the "water surrounded by a dike" can-
    not be better indicated than they are in the group
    nearer to the sign *"one stone."*
        The period of five years (1318–1324) which it
    took the Mexicans to settle and build their city, is
    just the one given in our Codex. The date "9 reed"
    (1318) coincides with the last footprint or final
    stop of the Mexicans, and the year "one stone"
    (1324) is in front of the white oak. These are pre-
    cisely the two dates given by the best authorities
    for the foundation of Mexico. The signs, though, are

to be related to the fourteenth century: The Indian painter, living in the fifteenth century, was as sure as we are now, by tradition, that the two dates were "nine *acatl*" and "one *tecpal*" but he could not be more precise, for as is pointed out, their method for discriminating the cycles, although theoretically good, was out of practice in the fifteenth century.

D. A period of twenty-two years was covered by the big war and conquest of the Tecpaneca lands. The two dominant figures, Itzcohuatl and Moctezuma, are embraced in it. The main political event, the Council of the Four selected noblemen, is clearly shown. Here they are seen having a regular session just in front of the date of their appointment, on the fifth year of Itzcohuatl's reign, 10 *acatl* (1437).

E. The final triumph of Moctezuma I, the "woman-like" ambassador, over his powerful enemies, is beautifully synthesized by the picture of a king in full robe and with hair, dressed like a woman but, nevertheless, on top of another much bigger king whose crown has been taken away. This symbolizes the events of the year 1457 as it appears in our Codex.

F. The names of towns written in Spanish characters, although of much later date, make us think that the second painter, or a commentarist, in the sixteenth century, had some vague idea that these three groups give a comprehensive view of that important war period. The towns whose names are still legible certainly were very closely connected with that war. Such are, for instance, Azcaputzalco, Talalpam (*sic*), Heichilputi (*sic*) (now Churubuzco), Tacahuaya (for Atlicuahuayan, now Tacubaya), Miahuatlan, and Tepeapulco.

G.   The next prominent figure in the Codex is King Netza-hualpilli just facing the year 1471 of his election. His hieroglyphic is most appropriately that of a "hungry child." The reasons for his appearance among the Mexican rulers were given in our previous notes in this commentary.

H.   Ahuitzotl, the monster of cruelty and his indelible national crime: the dedication of the two parallel shrines (Huitzilopochtli and Tezcalipuca) are plainly painted in the direction of the sign "10 rabbits" (1486), the very date given by the best historians.

On the upper part of the sheet, under the date "2 houses" (1533) a similar figure is given. Evidently it is not a picture of any actual event, as no Mexican ruler, no temples, no sacrifices had lasted after 1526. It is the picture of something that the *tecuilo* took for granted that was going to happen, if the ritual laws were to be kept; and, we add, if the Spanish conquest, which the *tecuilo* could not foresee, had not come to stop that rite or sacrifice. This anonymous king with his two temples ready for the sacrifice, is possibly the expression of the sac-rifice prescribed for the middle of the cycle, which had to occur precisely in 1533, or (1507–26) as it comes in our Codex.

Part II: Post-Cortesian

A. A Spanish *conquistador* of the beginning of the six-teenth century, riding on a horse (designed here by a hand probably used to painting only deer) is at-tacking, sword in hand, a Mexican Indian. Such a group by the year 1 *acatl* (1519), the very year of the arrival and first attacks of Cortés, can only be the expression of the Conquest of Mexico. Nothing justi-fies the importance here given to Tetlapulco, a vil-lage no more in existence, and where no battle took place. Is the conqueror here painted, a portrait of Hernán Cortés? There can be nothing but conjec-ture on this particular point.

B. It is certain that the famous Franciscan cross was first erected in 1526 when the missionaries moved from their little chapel (at the corner of what is now Argentina and Guatemala streets) to the site of their new church of San Francisco. The new pos-sessor of the Codex believed (and he was right) that such an important fact ought to be recorded. But he was not familiar with the old Aztec way of record-ing nor with the Spanish way either. So in a very childish but typical Indian fashion he expressed his date with the few figures he happened to know: (4 4 4 4 4 4 2=26). This probable explanation is confirmed by the similar method used to record the foundation of the town of San Marcos ($4\ 4\ 4\ 4\ 4\ 4\ 4=32$).

C. The painting of the holy Evangelist with his symbolic lion would not be of itself the sign of a town. But the *marqués* crown on top of the Saint has no meaning unless it refers to the Marquis of Salinas to whom this very town (some twenty miles north of the City of Mexico) had to pay annual tribute, as we know from the "Anales Franciscanos." The only reason we find for including the San Marcos foundation among the main events of the country, is that such a town was of great importance—for the painter.

D. *A Virgin with her hands folded near her heart, her head bent towards her right shoulder, dressed in a salmon colored tunic and a greenish blue mantilla (see the unique design as in the original) is the Virgin of Guadalupe as venerated in Tepeyac, four miles north of the City of Mexico, and some six miles south of San Marcos. By painting it a little lower than the year 1532 it is well indicated that her year was 1531.*

E. The bell seen as a part of the lost portion of the Codex is not of sufficient moment to warrant any serious consideration.

The Age of the Codex

The Codex Saville is especially important on account of its extraordinary antiquity among the historical codices of

America. At first glance, any expert archaeologist would refer the pre-Cortesian part of the Codex to the middle of the fifteenth century. A closer analysis leads us to the same conclusion for several good reasons:

1. Its paper is of the most primitive and rough material. There is nothing on it like the coating used by all the *tecuilos* of the end of the fifteenth century to smooth the surface and make it ready for painting.

2. The designs are genuinely simple, very different from those colorful and standardized gods and warriors so much in vogue in the time of Ahuitzotl 1486. The pre-Hispanic part, the only one we are referring to now, was designed with deep black vegetable ink. The colors are of that much later date when the *tecuilo* had lost even the notion that the *colpilli* or royal crowns were golden instead of blue.

3. Another sign of antiquity is the absence of more progressive writing. The oldest kind of script is called figurative. Its meaning is simply the painted design. At most it uses some natural sign, like footprints for human walking. The second kind is called ideographic, which expresses abstract ideas or verbs, as, for instance, a conventional curve line before the lips meaning to ask and another one to answer. The third kind of script, called phonetic, paints two or more things whose names if articulated sound like the name of a very different object. The last two ways of writing are not used at all in this Codex because they are of later invention. The Codex there-

fore is much older than the end of the fifteenth century.

4. The system of dating in our Codex is the same substantially as the one used by the other historical codices, but it is handled in a very awkward way. It only gives you the initial sign for every *tlalpilli* (period of thirteen years) leaving you the task of counting when you try to find a year. Now the need for improvements in chronology, as well as in any other human invention, is a natural proof of antiquity just as an oil lamp must be much older than an electric light.

5. We can go still further to a more certain and definite statement: The Codex was started before the year 1454 A.D. It is admitted by first-class historians that the "Feast of the Sacred Fire" which, according to civil and religious law, was to be celebrated at the end of the cycle, namely, in the year "13 houses" (1453), was transferred, owing to the necessary correction of the calendar, to the first morning of "2 reeds" (1455). Now the original writer when making his paradigm or frame of the vertical dating line with its circles, signs and symbols, painted the symbol of the cycle just in front of 1453.

When, later on, he knew of the correction of the calendar (that news must have been given some time before the end of 1453) he had to correct his time line as he did, by painting the symbol (a bundle of reeds) in 1455 and pasting a small piece of paper on top of the old one.[5] If he had to correct the mistake he made in 1453, he certainly made the mistake and did the painting in or before 1453. It is hard to tell how long before 1454 the Codex was in existence. From the details, though, of the Itzcóatl period, which seem to be taken from personal impressions of the *tecuilo* [i.e., himself—JBS], one feels inclined to believe that he began to write sometime around 1440. After we have reached this conclusion it is quite natural to ask: "Do you think this is the oldest book in America?" It is hard to tell; but if we take the word "book" in its formal sense, I think we can give an affirmative answer.

[5.] Orozco y Berra, *Historia antigua y de la Conquista de México*, vol. II, pp. 44, 45, 90, maintains that the correction took place in 1299. He tries to prove his statement by quoting the Tellerian and Vatican Codices, but the fact is, they do not show the original sign of the correction for that remote year. Perfect reproductions of them are in all good libraries.

The Apology of Mier

DECEMBER 12, 1794, WAS A FATEFUL DAY IN THE LIFE OF Servando Teresa de Mier, aristocrat and Dominican priest. On that feast day of Our Lady of Guadalupe he delivered a sermon at the Tepeyac sanctuary on his theory of the origin of the mysterious painting. Mier's view so inflamed the bishop of Mexico City that he was expelled from the country.

The exiled intellectual went first to Spain, then to England, where he remained for many years. The irony of his expulsion lies in the fact that he actually believed the cloak painting to be miraculous.

Mier's idea appears at once fascinating and preposterous. The Image of Guadalupe was a miracle, he said, but not one primarily involving an apparition to a sixteenth-century Christianized Aztec. The miraculous painting in his view, was far older, having been originally the property of an evangelizing Christian, whom the Indians called Quetzalcóatl!

The mythic legend of Quetzalcóatl is well known. The story involves a bearded white man visiting the Indians,

only to depart abruptly. The loss is lessened somewhat by
Quetzalcóatl's promise to return someday. Scholarship has
revealed that a real person, a Toltec king who called himself Topiltzin-Quetzalcóatl, did live at the end of the
tenth century. But how did Topiltzin acquire the name
Quetzalcóatl?

According to the thesis of Mier (which was borrowed
from the historian Ignacio Borunda), a bearded Jew had
made his way from distant India to Mexico about the sixth
century. This man, who was large by Indian standards,
spoke of himself as "Saint Thomas."

It was under the auspices of this "Saint Thomas" that
somehow (the details are lost) the Guadalupe cloak first
presented itself. If this account is true, the painting is a
thousand years older than generally thought and has no
more than a peripheral relationship with the Tepeyac
locale.

The tradition of associating Juan Diego's apparition of
Mary with the Madonna cloak is primarily Indian. The
Spanish colonists do not seem to have embraced the
belief for several decades and, in any event, codices reproduced elsewhere in this book clearly originate as Indian
memory. If by Mier's time the Church was able to exile
one of its own for merely expressing public doubt concerning the received tradition, this only illustrates the
extent to which the creoles now considered themselves
specifically Mexican, not European.

As the Guadalupan tradition was becoming stronger,
another Indian legend was becoming favorably, if somewhat reluctantly, assessed. This was the legend relating

Quetzalcóatl and Saint Thomas, which Mier had resurrected in 1794. The idea had never gained wide notice, but as Mier himself indicated, it had been carefully preserved by the intelligentsia: "I was not surprised by this preaching, for I had heard about it from infancy from the mouth of my learned father. All that I have since learned has confirmed its existence, and I do not believe a single cultured American does not know about it or doubts it."[1]

Mier's claim is confirmed in the testimony of several different regions and strengthened in that the different titles suggest independent traditions: "Bochica" is cited in Colombia, "Viracocha" in Peru, "Zume" in Brazil and in Paraguay. In nearer Mayan Yucatan, the name given was "Kulkulkan."[2] The historian Juan de Tovar (see "The Primitive Relation," above) was instrumental in the ignition of the Quetzalcóatl-Saint Thomas tradition. Written in the last quarter of the sixteenth century, his *History* calls specific attention to it. "For a better understanding of this," he observes, "it must be remembered that long ago there lived in this country a man who, according to tradition, was a great saint and came to this land to announce the Holy Gospel."[3]

[1] Servando Teresa de Mier, *Memorias* (Mexico City: 1946), vol. 1, p. 5; cited in Jacques Lafaye, *Quetzalcóatl and Guadalupe*, trans. Benjamin Keen (Chicago: University of Chicago Press, 1976).

[2] Lafaye, op. cit., p. 190.

[3] Juan de Tovar, *Manuscrit Tovar: Origines et croyances des Indiens du Mexique*, ed. Jacques Lafaye (Graz, Austria: Akademische Druck- und Verlagsanstalt, for UNESCO, 1972), p. 69; cited in Lafaye, *Quetzalcóatl*, p. 163.

Some one hundred years later, following the inquiry of
1666 in which he had testified (see Chapter II), mathematics professor Bercero Tanco appears to have been the
first person directly linking the Saint Thomas legend with
that of the Virgin of Guadalupe. His testimony was later
published in book form, selections from which follow in
the Appendices.

Just a few years later, Manuel Duarte payed tribute to
Tanco's work with the Saint Thomas legend: "In order
that you may know that he was in New Spain, read *The
Apparition of the Virgin of Guadalupe,* printed in Mexico
in 1675 . . . There you will see that Saint Thomas was in
Tula [a town north of Guadalupe], as is clearly shown by
the Bachiller Bercero, professor of the Mexican language,
who read about it in the Indian histories which tell of the
prodigious works and the doctrines taught by this
Ketzalcohuatl . . . In 1680, when I returned to the
Philippines, I left a manuscript notebook of more than
fifty-two sheets, containing information relative to the
teaching of the apostle Saint Thomas in New Spain with
the Bachiller Don Carlos de Siguenza, professor of
mathematics."[4]

These were the sheets which the historian Lorenzo
Beneducci Boturini laboriously reassembled about 1745:
"Moreover, I have historical notes on the preaching of
the glorious apostle Saint Thomas in America. These are
contained in thirty-four China papers which, I suppose,

[4] Manuel Duarte, in Nicolas León, *Bibliografía Mexicana del siglo
XVIII* (Mexico City: 1902–8), "Pulma rica," pp. 500–14; cited in
Lafaye, *Quetzalcóatl*, pp. 187, 191.

were used by Don Carlos de Siguenza in writing a book on the same subject."[5]

This returns us to the general period in which Borunda and Mier were beginning to work, the late eighteenth century. Recalling with Tovar that "those who found a tan skin in a village on the Gulf coast" were the same people who believed that Saint Thomas made an early mission to Mexico,[6] we must recognize the fact that almost every Indian record had been destroyed by the conquistadors. These ancient codices bore no words, for the early Indians employed picture writing exclusively. To European eyes, the codices were caricatures if not blasphemies. Bishop Zumárraga himself consigned great numbers to public bonfires.

Borunda believed that these Mexican hieroglyphics contained information quite unknown to any one but the former inhabitants of Anahuac, the ancient Aztec empire. I reproduce from his rare work, *General Key to American Hieroglyphics*:

Concerning the figurative writings of really unknown signs . . . the eagle of the Church, an African bishop . . . flourishing at the end of the fourth century [Saint Augustine of Hippo?] . . . warned that the great remedy is the

[5.] Lorenzo Benaducci Boturini, *Catálogo del Museo Indiano del Cavallero Boturini* (Mexico City: Library of the Basilica de Guadalupe, n.d.). See also Lafaye, *Quetzalcóatl.*
[6.] "It was a very ancient tanned skin on which were shown in Mexican hieroglyphics all the mysteries of our faith, though mixed with many errors." Tovar, *Manuscrit Tovar*, p. 73; cited in Lafaye, *Quetzalcóatl*, pp. 163–64.

remedy of language . . . encouraging [us] to penetrate symbols or signals as—an animal, by its smell, fire by its smoke, and so forth—as many things giving more delight to truth when discovered through images and symbols.

[The Indians] invented significant hieroglyphics . . . not with letters but with sculptured figures . . . [the result is that] hieroglyphics [are arranged] in such a manner that sacred ideas can be expressed, whereas . . . languages of various nations would be unable to adequately convey these intentions.

When we are thus soaked in our own literal writing, gradually perfected in the space of many centuries, we do not remember the particular style which would make understandable concepts which were familiar in terms of ancient characters. We are left today with paradoxical inconsistencies, such as one equal to ten; another to fifteen; and yet another, to twenty.

And in this regard we are aware that it is declared, in the Orient, without the likelihood of explanation in terms of communication from Europe or the Occident and still much less from New Spain, that it was initially in Mylapore [modern Madras] ancient capital of the coast of Coromandel and the Gulf of Bengal, the same named by the Portuguese "Canamina," in allusion to the canes [hieroglyphics] . . . that they were using in ancient times.[7]

Here we have the basis for Mier's alternative history of the Guadalupe Image. The Dominican believed that Saint Thomas of Mylapore, India, introduced the Gospel into ancient Mexico. The Incarnation necessarily involves

[7.] Ignacio Borunda, *Clave general de jeroglíficos americanos* (Mexico City: Library of the Basilica de Guadalupe, n.d.), pp. 14–19.

the sacred relationship between Mother and Son. The cloak bearing the Madonna portrait belonged to Saint Thomas and had remained generation after generation a signal reminder of the Christian who had come from the East.

The connection of the Image on the cloak with Tepeyac hill, Mier asserted, had little to do with a baptized Aztec renamed "Juan Diego." This hill had been for centuries a favorite place of worship for the Indians, a fact which almost certainly lay at the root of sixteenth-century Franciscan opposition to the Guadalupan cultus such as that of the missionary-historian Bernardino de Sahagún. "Now that the church of Our Lady of Guadalupe has been built," he wrote, "the Indians also call her 'Tonantzin,' on the pretext that the preachers call Our Lady, the Mother of God, 'Tonantzin' . . . This is an abuse which should be stopped, for the true name of the Mother of God is not Tonantzin, but Dios-Nantzin, 'God' and 'nantzin' . . . The Indians today, as in the old days, come from afar to visit this Tonantzin . . ."[8] Sahagún's objection was that the unique status of Mother of God (Dios-nantzin) was diluted by being equated with Our Mother (Tonantzin, the Aztec goddess).

Mier, on the other hand, believed the connection between Tonantzin and the Virgin Mary to have been made centuries before—in the times of Saint Thomas-Quetzalcóatl. If that was so, there was no abuse by the sixteenth-

8. Bernardino de Sahagún, *Historia general de las cosas de la Nueva España*, 4 vols. (Mexico City: Porrúa, 1956), vol. III, p. 352; cited in Lafaye, *Quetzalcóatl*, p. 216.

century Indians. They were only doing what they had always done. Although they did not remember her as such, Tonantzin, gradually distorted through the centuries, was originally both Our Lady and the Mother of God, Mary:

> Who then was this Tonantzin or Tzenteotenantzin whom Quetzalcoatl taught the Indians to know and who from those remote times had been venerated on Tepeyac hill, also named Tonantzin? She was a virgin, consecrated to God, in the service of the Temple, who by the will of heaven conceived and bore . . . the Lord with the Crown of Thorns, Teohuitznahuac, who partook of both human and divine natures.[9]

Mier is pointing to the several corresponding roles shared by Tonantzin and by the Virgin Mary. His ultimate point, however, is that the Guadalupe cloak dates from a period far earlier than the sixteenth century. Given the legends of ancient voyagers to America—Irish Saint Brendan in the sixth century and Welsh Prince Madoc in the twelfth century—plus parallel tradition by the Mormons, decoding any symbolic significance abiding in the Image of Guadalupe becomes desirable. Perhaps carbon-14 testing on the tilma to determine its age, until now considered unnecessary on the presumption that the tilma could not be more than four hundred and fifty years old, would shed some light on the matter.

---

[9] Servando Teresa de Mier, "Manifesto apologético," in *Escritos inéditos* (Mexico City: Library of the Basilica de Guadalupe, n.d.). See also Mier, "Apología del Dr. Mier," in *Memorias*, vol. 1, pp. 37–38; cited in Lafaye, *Quetzalcóatl*.

Bercero Tanco:
Proofs of the Apparition[1]

THE NEWS THAT EXISTS IN THIS CITY ABOUT THE APPARITION
of Our Lady, and of the origin of her miraculous Image,
which is called Guadalupe, remains more vividly in the
memory of the Indians because, it was to Indians that she
first manifested herself. Consequently, they recorded it,
and kept it as a memorable event in all their papers and
writings. As among other traditions of their ancestors, so
it is also necessary to establish first of all the level of belief
which should be given to all their writings and memoirs.

The natives (particularly the Mexicans) had two systems of preserving their history, laws, judicial matters, and
traditions of their elders, in [much] the same way the
Western world does it.

One was by means of paintings of the events which
depict them. These paintings were made quite vividly on

1. Bercero Tanco, *Felicity of Mexico* (Mexico City: private edition
for D. Felipe de Zuñiga y Ontiveros, 1780), pp. 36–52. Here
translated by Jody Smith.

coarse paper (*papel de estraza*), deer or other animal skins, which were tanned and prepared for this purpose in the manner of a soft papironn, and on each of these "canvases" they painted on the top, the bottom, on the sides, the signs of the years of each one of their centuries; which consisted of fifty-two solar years, and each year of three hundred sixty-five days. The natural months consisted of one full moon to the next (as the Hebrew has), and so they have only one name, which is Metzli.

But for all their rites, ceremonies, and sacrifices to their false deities, as well as for their festivities, the year had eighteen months of twenty days each, which amounts to three hundred sixty days, and after these had passed they added five, which they called "intercals," in the manner of our leap years, which did not belong to any month in the year.

They also painted the characters corresponding to the months and years in which the events took place, as well as the characters and figures corresponding to the King and the Lords under which such events took place.

These paintings were and still are as authentic as the writings of our scribes, because they did not trust ignorant people, but only the priests and historians whose authority and credibility was greatly appreciated during the times of the Gentilisimo; so there is little doubt about the veracity of such recordings (characters and paintings); since they have to be exposed to the viewing of everybody in each century, inaccuracy would result in a loss of prestige by the priests. So if we discard the superstitions and rites in honor of their false deities, to whom they attributed some happy or unhappy events, the historical part is authentic and true.

The second form which the natives used to preserve their memorable events and to be transmitted from generation to generation was by means of songs (cantatas) composed by the same priests, with certain types of verse with some voacables added only to preserve a certain rhythm. These cantatas were taught to children who had certain abilities such as memory and musicality and who, upon reaching a certain age as well as proficiency, sang them during their festivities and celebrations, accompanied by teponaztles.

Through these songs, traditions and events older than five hundred and a thousand years passed from one generation to the next. Wars, victories, misfortunes, hungers, plague, births and deaths of Kings and Lords were related; The beginning and end of different dynasties and all memorable events were thus described.

From those maps, paintings, characters and songs, the Rev. Fr. Juan de Torquemada drew his sources for the writing of the first volume of his *Indian Monarchy*, in which he relates the foundation of this City of Mexico, as well as many other older things, [such as] the life and death of all those who governed these Kingdoms before the advent of the Spaniards.

The learned natives continued this same way of writing their history, even after they became subjects of the Crown of Castille, where they conform with the Spanish historians. And after the Indians learned to read and write the Spanish, many Indians continued writing in their Mexican language all the important events which were happening, as well as the old ones which they copied from their maps and paintings.

The members of Spanish religious orders used all these paintings to write about the history of the Land, believing them to be accurate and believing them to be true.

It is well known that the Franciscan monks founded in their convent in Santiago Tlaltelolco, a college in which many Indian children learned to read and write the Spanish language, Music, and Latin grammar and Rhetoric, as well as other Liberal Arts subjects. These children became well-learned and worthy men, and they were the ones who showed the Spanish (our people) the way they should interpret their drawings and symbols, and also, how to compute their centuries, years, months and days, and terms of numbers and figures.

From this we may infer that the Tlaxcaltecan and Acolhua Indians were the most intelligent and clever in the New World, although they also were the ones who were the most influenced by the rites and ceremonies with which they adored their false deities by means of the most cruel sacrifices.

Based on all these things I say and affirm, that among all the memorable events that the well-learned and wise Indians from the college of Santa Cruz (who were in the majority the sons of Nobles and Lords) painted in their former way for those who did not know how to read and write our alphabet; and with the letters of our alphabet for those who knew how to read them, [they affirmed] the miraculous apparition of Our Lady of Guadalupe as well as the painting of her Sacred image.

I certify to have seen and read an important and very old map written by the Indians with figures and signs in which they narrated events that took place more than three hundred year before the coming of the Spaniards to this land. This map with some lines added, with letters but in the Mexican language, was in the possession of D. Fernando de Alva [Ixtlilxochitl], who was the interpreter of the Indian Tribunal of the Viceroys, and who was a very wise and learned man who spoke and understood very well the Mexican language and who knew well the way of interpreting the paintings and characters of the Indians. Since he was a descendent, on his mother's side of the King of Texcoco, he inherited and had in his possession many maps and historical papers in which all the events which took place during the lives of his ancestors were recorded.

And among the events related after the "pacification" of this Kingdom and City of Mexico, was the one about the miraculous apparition of Our blessed Lady of Guadalupe.

He also had in his position a notebook written in Spanish and the Mexican language, by one of the most capable Indians from the College of Santa Cruz, in which the four apparitions to Juan Diego were related, as well as the fifth one, to his uncle Juan Bernadino.

The second way used by the Indians to preserve for posterity the important events were the cantatas, which I affirm and certify to have heard the old Indians [sing] during their religious ceremonies which they used to have before the flood of the Indian city and, when they celebrated the ceremonies in honor of Our Lady of Guadalupe in her Sacred Temple and in the Plaza which faced the West side of the Church cemetary. Many dancers formed a circle and in the middle two old ones sung, accompanied by teponaztli, the cantata that referred to the apparition of the Holy Virgin, and which also told about the cloak or tilma, which was Juan Diego's cape, how it manifested itself to Juan de Zumárraga, first bishop of this City. At the end of the contata, [were told] the miracles that the Lord had performed the day the Image of Our Lady was placed in her first hermitage and the joyful celebration by the Indians. And this was the end of the oldest and true tradition.

Annals of Bartolache

THIS IS ONE OF THE ANNALS FOUND BY DR. JOSÉ IGNACIO Bartolache in 1787 in the library of the University of Mexico. These annals cover the period from 1454 to 1737. The references to Our Lady of Guadalupe are the following:

13 caña, 1531: The Castilians walked the ground of Cuetlaxcoapan, city of Los Angeles (puebla) and to Juan Diego was manifested the beloved Lady of Guadalupe in Mexico, at the place named Tepeyac.
Pedernal year, 1548: Juan Diego, to whom appeared the Blessed Lady of Guadalupe, died.[1]

[1] P. Feliciano Velázquez, *The Apparition of St. Mary of Guadalupe* (Mexico City: Patricio Sanz, 1931); cited in *Guadalupan Documentation: 1531–1768* (Mexico City: Centro de Estudios Guadalupanos, 1980), p. 109.

Reply of Fr. Juan de Tovar[1]

This is a reply by Fr. Juan de Tovar (c. 1546–1626) to questions raised by Fr. José de Acosta (c. 1539–1600) concerning the degree of validity assignable to the Indian codices in light of the Indians' lack of an alphabet. Tovar's answer is illuminating on the entire matter of Guadalupan origins.

ALTHOUGH I COULD HAVE ANSWERED AS SOON AS I RECEIVED your letter and could have given a solution to what you ask, nevertheless I was so anxious for the history to find favor with you that I wanted to refresh my memory more diligently. I communicated with some old Indian chiefs of Tula, who are wise in these matters, very learned in this language, and much like the old chiefs of Mexico and Texcoco, with whom I made the history in this way. Viceroy Don Martin Enriquez, wishing to know these peoples antiquities exactly, ordered a collection of the libraries that they had on these matters. The people of Mexico, Texcoco, and Tula brought them, since these people were the historians and sages in these matters. The Viceroy sent the papers and books to me with Dr. Portillo, formerly vicar general of this Archbishopric, charging me to examine

[1] George Kubler and Charles Gibson, *Tovar Calendar*, Memoirs of the Connecticut Academy of Arts and Sciences, vol. XI (New Haven: Yale University Press, 1951), pp. 77–78.

and study them, and to make some relation to be sent to the king . . .

I looked over all this history, the characters and hieroglyphs of which I did not understand. Therefore it was necessary for the wise men of Mexico, Texcoco, and Tula to meet with me, by order of the Viceroy. Talking over and discussing the matter in detail with them, I made a thorough history, which, when it was finished, was taken by Dr. Portillo, who promised to make two copies with very fine pictures, one for the king and one for us. At this juncture, it happened that he went to Spain, and he was never able to make good his word, nor were we able to retrieve the history. But as I had then investigated and discussed the matter at great length, it remained in my strongly in my memory. In addition, I saw a book made by a Dominican friar, a relative of mine, which was very similar to the ancient library that I had seen, and which helped me to refresh my memory in making the history that you have now read. I put down what was most certain, and omitted other dubious small matters, and this is the authority that it has, a great authority in my opinion, since in addition to what I saw in their own books, I discussed it, prior to the cocolistle, with all the old men whom I knew to have knowledge of it. No one disagreed, a rare circumstance among them. This is what I answer to your first question, concerning the authority of this history.

To the second question, how could the Indian retain so many things in their memory without writing, I repeat that they had figures and hieroglyphs with which they painted things in this way. Objects that could be represented *directly* were drawn in their own image. Whatever could not be represented directly was drawn with characters *representing* an image. In this way they [the Indians] drew what they wished. And as for their remembering the time in which each event took place, you have already read about the computation that these people used, how they made each fifty-two years a wheel, as I mentioned there. The wheel was like a century, and with these wheels they preserved the memory of the times in which the memorable events occurred, painting the events at the sides of the wheels with the characters mentioned. The wheels and circles of the years that I saw numbered four, since these people have no other count. From the time that they left the seven caves, mentioned at the beginning of that history, until the Spaniard came, three complete wheels had passed and the fourth was in progress. In these wheels all the events and memorable occurrences were indicated, as you will see in the wheel and the end of the calendar that goes with this. There they put the Spaniard with red coat and hat, as an indication of the time when the Spaniards entered this land. This was in the fourth wheel or age, during the sign that they call reed, which they painted in the form that you will see there. But it is to be noted that although they had different figures and characters with which they wrote, their method was less adequate than our writing, in which everyone knows verbatim what was written by the very words. They [the Indians] agreed only in the concepts.

But the words and forms of the "orators' speeches and the many songs composed by the orators were known by all without any disagreement, even though they pictured them with their characters. In order to preserve the words that the orators and poets spoke, they held an exercise every day in the colleges of the young chiefs who were to succeed them, and with this continual repetition, the most famous orations of each time remained in their memory. This was a system for impressing the young with the fact that they were to be rhetoricians, and in this manner many orations were preserved verbatim from generation to generation until the Spaniards came. The Spaniards wrote in our letters many orations and songs that I saw, and thus they have been preserved. This is the answer to the last question, how it was possible to have this memory of the words, etc. And to add to what I have said here, I sent to you the orations of the Pater Noster, etc., and of the general confession, and other matters of our faith, as the ancients wrote and learned them by their characters, which were sent to me by the old men of Texcoco and Tula. And this will be enough to show in what manner the ancients wrote their histories and orations. Also I sent, besides the calendar of the Indians, another, very curious, in which their months and days and fiestas are equated with the fiestas and months and year of our ecclesiastical calendar. Certainly it excites admiration to see that these Indians achieved so much with their cleverness and skill, as you will see by these papers that I send."

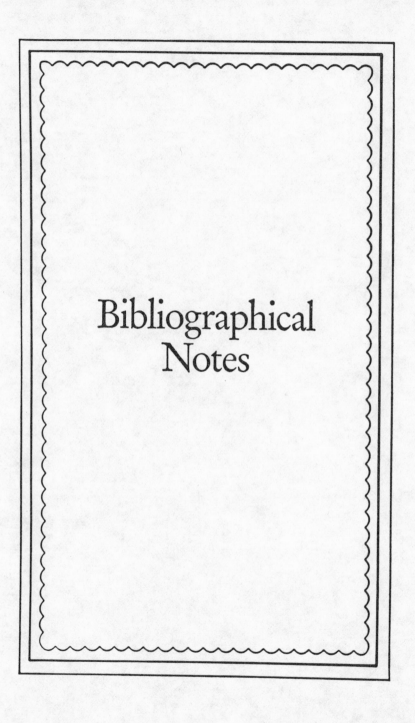

Bibliographical
Notes

Bibliographical
Notes

I. Our Lady of Guadalupe

Demarest, Donald, and Taylor, Coley B., eds., *The Dark Virgin: The Book of Our Lady of Guadalupe* (New York: The Devin-Adair Co., 1956).

Eliot, Ethel Cook, "Guadalupe" in John J. Delaney, ed., *A Woman Clothed with the Sun* (Garden City, N.Y.: Doubleday & Company, 1961), pp. 39–60.

Hawkins, Columbine, "Our Lady of Guadalupe—Miracle of Iconography" (Lafayette, Ore.: Trappist Abbey of Our Lady of Guadalupe, 1951).

Laso de la Vega, Luis, *Bachiller, Huey Tlamahuicoltica Omonexiti in ilhuicac Tlatoca cihuapilli Santa Maria,— Iotlaconantzin Guadalupe in nican huei altapenahuac Mexico itocayocan Tepeyacac* (Mexico City, 1649). English translation by Cleofas Calleros, M.F.A., in Harold J. Rahm, *Am I Not Here?* (Washington, N.J.: Ave Maria Institute, 1962), pp. 142, 144.

López-Beltrán, Lauro, "Guadalupanismo Internacional" in *La Virgen de Guadalupe*, special edition of *Mexico Desconocido* (Mexico City: Editorial Novaro, 1981), pp. 29–32.

Northrop, F. S. C., *The Meeting of East and West* (New York: The Macmillan Company, 1946), pp. 25–26.

Orozco, José Luis, "La Guadalupana en la Batalla de Lepanto?" in *La Virgen de Guadalupe*, pp. 19–20.

Rahm, Harold J., *Am I Not Here?* (Washington, N.J.: Ave Maria Institute, 1962), pp. 142, 144.

Sánchez, Miguel, *Imagen de la Virgen María, Madre de Dios de Guadalupe milagrosamente aparecida en México* (Mexico City, 1648).

II. Not Made with Human Hands

Behrens, Helen, tr., *The Virgin and the Serpent-God* (Mexico City: Editorial Progreso, 1966), pp. 170–74, for report of Rivera's examination of the painting. Also see Harold J. Rahm, op. cit., pp. 60–61, 69, 70.

Cabrera, Miguel, *Maravilla Americana—y conjunto de Raras Maravillas Observadas con la dirección de las reglas del arte de la pintura en la prodigiosa Imagen de nuestra Sra. de Guadalupe de México* (Mexico City, 1756), (Mexico City: Editorial Jus, second edition, 1977), chapter VII, pp. 18–22. English translation from Donald Demarest and Coley B. Taylor, op. cit., pp. 153–55.

Cuevas, Mariano, "The Codex Saville/Tetlapalco" from *Catholic Historical Records and Studies,* U. S. Catholic Historical Society, N.Y., 1929, vol. XIX, in Donald Demarest and Coley B. Taylor, eds., op. cit., pp. 168 ff.

Demarest, Donald, and Taylor, Coley B., eds., *The Dark Virgin: The Book of Our Lady of Guadalupe* (New York: The Devin-Adair Co., 1956).

Florencia, Francisco de, *La Estrella del Norte* (Madrid, 1688), quoted in Donald Demarest and Coley B. Taylor, op. cit., pp. 156, 157, 160.

Garibay-Kintana, Ángel María, *La Maternidad Espiritual de María* (Mexico City, 1961), in Helen Behrens, tr., *The Virgin and the Serpent-God* (Mexico City: Editorial Progreso, 1966), pp. 183, 184.

Irenaeus, Saint, *Against Heresies,* Book III, Chapter 21, No. 7, in Alexander Roberts and James Donaldson (ed. and tr.), *The Ante-Nicene Fathers,* vol. II (Grand Rapids, Mich.: William D. Eerdmans Publishing Co., 1962–66).

Motolinia, Toribio de, *Información de 1556,* in F. de Jesús Chauvet, *El Culto Guadalupano del Tepeyac* (Mexico

City: Centro de Estudios Bernardino de Sahagún, sixth edition, 1978), pp. 212–51.

New Catholic Encyclopedia, 1965 edition, vol. IV, pp. 821–22.

Rojas, Mario, *Segundo Encuentro Guadalupano* (Mexico City, 1978).

Sahagún, Bernardino de, *Historia General, 1559–1567,* III, 352, quoted in Jacques Lafaye, *Quetzalcóatl and Guadalupe* (Chicago: The University of Chicago Press, 1976), Benjamin Keen, tr., p. 216.

Salinas, Carlos, and De la Mora, Manuel, *Descubrimiento de un Busto Humano en las ojos de la Virgen María de Guadalupe* (Mexico City: Editorial Tradición, 1976), pp. 52, 54, 56–58.

Ugarte, José Bravo, *Cuestiones Guadalupanas* (Mexico City, 1946), Part I.

Wilson, Ian, *The Shroud of Turin* (Garden City, N.Y.: Doubleday & Company, revised edition, 1979), p. 115.

III. Impossible Coincidences

Jung, Carl Gustav, *The Structure and Dynamics of the Psyche,* Bollingen Series XX, Vol. 8 (Princeton, N.J.: Princeton University Press, second edition, 1969), p. 441.

Lafaye, Jacques, *Quetzalcóatl and Guadalupe* (Chicago: University of Chicago Press, 1976), Benjamin Keen, tr.

IV. In Search of Mary

Augustine of Hippo, Saint, *On the Trinity, Patrologia Latina,* V, 42:8.

Brownrigg, Robert, *Who's Who in the New Testament* (New York: Pillar Books, 1971), p. 344.

De Clari, Robert, *The Conquest of Constantinople* (New York: Columbia University Press, 1936), Edgar H. McNeal, tr., pp. 89, 126.

Eusebius of Caesarea, *Ecclesiastical History* (Cambridge, Mass.: Harvard University Press, 1926 and 1932), Vol. 1 tr. by Kirsopp Lake; Vol. 2 tr. by J. E. L. Oulton.

Forsyth, Ilene H., *The Throne of Wisdom: Wood Sculptures of the Madonna in Romanesque France* (Princeton, N.J.: Princeton University Press, 1972), p. 10.

Gibbon, Edward, *Decline and Fall of the Roman Empire* (New York: The Modern Library, 1932), vol. III, p. 1116.

Grabar, André, *Christian Iconography* (Princeton, N.J.: Princeton University Press, 1961), p. 68.

Graves, Robert, and Patai, Raphael, *Hebrew Myths: The Book of Genesis* (Garden City, N.Y.: Doubleday & Company, 1964), p. 64.

Gregorovius, Ferdinand, *Athen und Athenais* (Dresden, 1887).

Jameson, Anna Brownell, *Legends of the Madonna, as Represented in the Fine Arts* (London: Hutchinson & Company, 1852), p. 25.

Lacurdhas, V., ed., *Photius Homiliai* (Thessalonika, Greece: Etaireia Makedhonikon Spoudhon, 1959), p. 45, fourth homily.

V. The Image Lost and Found

Boturini, Lorenzo Beneducci, *Idea de una nueva historia general de la América Septentrional* (Madrid, 1746), Dedication to the King, quoted in Lafaye, op. cit., pp. 248, 262, 268.

Camarge, Rosario, "*Modelo Preferido de los Artistas,*" in *La Virgen de Guadalupe*, p. 22.

Lafaye, Jacques, *Quetzalcóatl and Guadalupe* (Chicago: University of Chicago Press, 1976), Benjamin Keen, tr., p. 220.

Michener, James A., *Iberia* (New York: Random House, 1968), pp. 439–42.

Motolinia, Toribio de, *History of the Indians of New Spain* (Westport, Conn.: Greenwood Press, 1972), Elizabeth A. Foster, tr.

Northrop, F. S. C., op. cit., p. 28.

Sánchez-Flores, Ramón, "Actuales Investigaciones Históricas del Suceso Guadalupano," in *La Virgen de Guadalupe*, p. 41.

Tyler, R., tr., *The Monastery of Guadalupe* (Barcelona, 1930), p. 4.

VI. The Right Eye of the Virgin

Aste-Tonsmann, José, "Análisis por Computadora en los Ojos de la Virgen de Guadalupe," in *La Virgen de Guadalupe*, pp. 42–44.

Salinas, Carlos, and De la Mora, Manuel, op. cit., pp. 8–11, 16–18, 23–25, 33, 101.

VII. Science and the Miraculous

Callahan, Philip Serna, and Smith, Jody Brant, *The Virgin of Guadalupe: An Infrared Study* (Washington, D.C.: CARA, 1981). Spanish translation, Mexico City, by F. Faustino-Cervantes, 1981. Unless otherwise indicated, all quotations in this chapter are from this source, and were written by Dr. Callahan.

VIII. The Living Image

Bulgakov, Sergius, *A Bulgakov Anthology* (Philadelphia: Westminster Press, 1976), James Pain and N. Zernov, eds. and trs., pp. 10–11.

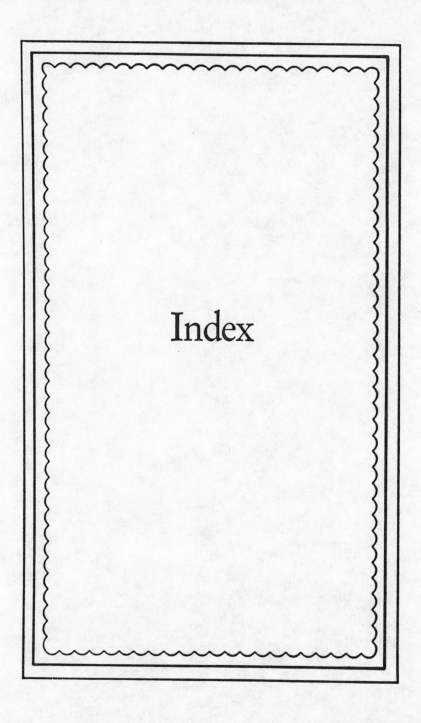

Index

JODY BRANT SMITH is associate professor of philosophy and religion at Pensacola Junior College in Florida. He is the author of several philosophical monographs, and co-author, with Philip Serna Callahan, of *The Virgin of Guadalupe: An Infrared Study*.